D0904875

Instructional television
status and directions

Instructional television

status and directions

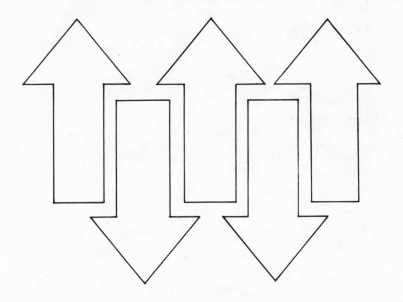

Jerrold Ackerman and Lawrence Lipsitz

editors

Educational Technology Publications
Englewood Cliffs, New Jersey 07632

WILLIAM MADISON RANDALL LIBRARY UNC AT WILMINGTON

Library of Congress Cataloging in Publication Data

Main entry under title:

Instructional television.

"Chapters in this volume appeared originally in the May 1976 issue of Educational technology."
Bibliography: p.
1. Television in education. I. Ackerman, Jerrold. II. Lipsitz, Lawrence. III. Educational technology.
LB1044.7.I492 , 371.33'58 76-54241
ISBN 0-87778-096-X

Copyright © 1977 Educational Technology Publications, Inc., Englewood Cliffs, New Jersey 07632.

All rights reserved. No part of this book may be reproduced or transmitted, in any form or by any means, electronic or mechanical, including photocopying, recording, or by any information storage and retrieval system, without permission in writing from the Publisher.

Printed in the United States of America.

Library of Congress Catalog Card Number:
76-54241.

International Standard Book Number:
0-87778-096-X.

First Printing: January, 1977.

LB1044
.7
.I492

Preface

There were *initial expectancies* concerning television's instructional possibilities which have not been realized. This book was motivated by recent developments in ITV hardware, software and the instructional systems which develop and use ITV programs. Accordingly, the volume discusses these: (1) initial expectancies, (2) shortcomings, and (3) recent developments and their implications.

For the reader who is relatively unfamiliar with the history of televised instruction, this present series of chapters should provide a broad overview. The educational technologist should take heart in the implications of recent developments, described in this book, although a favorable prognosis is by no means unanimous, as the reader of the following chapters will soon discover.

Organization of the Book

Vladimir K. Zworykin's keynote chapter makes clear that *television* hasn't failed. If there has been failure, it belongs to those responsible for its programming and use. The Zworykin chapter questions the indispensability of conventional educational systems. Such a notion has been gaining considerable momentum among educational technologists, and variations of this theme are sounded in several of the chapters which follow (e.g., Berkman, McBride, Perrin, Carl).

Donald G. Perrin's chapter summarizes in non-technical

163129

language the past history and current status of television's role in education. This background information supplies context illuminating the chapters which follow.

Diana R. Carl presents many of the issues involved in ITV program development. An understanding of ITV's current status requires knowledge of the type provided by Carl.

Gavriel Salomon offers a sample of the current work in cognitive psychology which seems destined to exert profound influence upon the theoretical structures of instructional media, particularly television. The relationships between symbolic codes, cognitive effects, instructional effectiveness and learning are explained. Salomon formalizes an hypothesis which may allow us to predict whether a particular attribute in an ITV program will be instructionally effective.

Paul Bosner offers a critical appraisal of ITV's status in what he sees as a massive, decentralized educational system characterized by fragmented funding structures and "obscured centers of power."

Jack McBride documents the history, purpose and organization of two related open learning delivery systems. The SUN (State University of Nebraska) and UMA (University of Mid-America) projects are working models of alternative learning systems (alternative to traditional schoolroom based learning).

Linda S. Agler and Theodore W. Pohrte describe how the Dallas County Community College District is now serving 10,000 students annually with systematically designed and produced instructional programs broadcast over open-circuit public television.

Frederick Williams and Monty C. Stanford examine the critical and multi-faceted roles of the evaluation component of ITV.

Dave Berkman is resolute in his conviction that the opportunity for exercising TV's instructional potentials has irretrievably passed—at least for the in-school system of education.

Richard W. Burns explains that instructionally effective TV

involves a total systems effort. Twenty-five elements which require purposeful attention in program planning are identified and described. Burns also develops the relationship between unique attributes of the medium and the selection of instructional objectives.

Rudy Bretz discusses hardware developments which were not available during the "first chance" period for *in-school* television.

E.W. Schneider focuses on the videodisc, which has the promise of low cost, accessibility and potential instructional flexibility. For all of his enthusiams, Schneider advises caution: videodisc technology may be ready for education, but are educational systems ready for the videodisc? Unfortunately, the entire maelstrom of issues swirling around the "software" and "systems of education" problems explored in this volume affect the instructional destiny of even the most ingenious hardware.

George N. Gordon, like Dave Berkman, takes a pessimistic view of ITV's "second chance" possibilities.

The final chapter, "Improving ITV's Instructional Image," by Jerrold Ackerman, introduces some organizing concepts for improving the status of ITV.

An Appendix, by Warren F. Seibert, describes recent research in important areas of instructional television.

The chapters in this volume appeared originally in the May, 1976 issue of *Educational Technology* magazine, with the exception of Chapter 7, which was published in the October, 1976 issue of the magazine. Chapter 14 is a considerably expanded version of the original magazine article. The research Appendix is used with the permission of the ERIC Clearinghouse on Information Resources at Stanford University.

Jerrold Ackerman
Lawrence Lipsitz
November, 1976

Table of Contents

Instructional television

status and directions

1.

Keynote to Volume:
A Challenge to Dream

Vladimir K. Zworykin

It has become popular in many areas, including educational ones, to criticize television for "not living up to its potential." Like most cliches, this one also misses the mark.

TV has shown us the moon, the planets and the stars. On earth, it has brought into our homes and our schools man at his best and at his worst. It has shown us our democracy in some of its finest and in some of its poorest hours. Yes, and it has distracted, bored and even insulted us.

These faults, however, are not inherent in television. Rather, television's failings can be ascribed for the most part to the people responsible for its programming. And, of course, since our main concern in this volume is the use of TV in education, I must point out that the failings in this area rest in good measure on those persons responsible for how instructional TV is used and programmed.

Therefore, I would like to issue a challenge to educators concerned with TV. Match the ingenuity and innovation of the engineers and scientists who developed television's technology; do not be afraid to dream about going beyond the confines of the known, the conventional and the convenient in your use of television for education. Do these things and you will destroy the cliche.

Vladimir K. Zworykin, widely recognized as the "Father of Television," is Honorary Vice President of RCA and Technical Consultant to RCA Laboratories.

To begin with, I suggest you ask yourself this question: Do we need conventional schools, classrooms and campuses to use television to its fullest educational potential?

There are two technological developments, in what might be called the gestation period, that could have a profound effect on educational methods, or perhaps I should say, on education itself. With proper utilization and management, these two developments could be used at any time, at any place and for a variety of educational and applied purposes.

One is the use of satellites to transmit TV signals directly to TV receivers in every corner of the globe. The other is the prerecording of TV programs on inexpensive discs, similar to phonograph records, that can play directly into any television receiver.

Satellite television will have its primary educational role, I believe, in the so-called developing nations, where there are very few, if any, costly TV transmitting stations, and, for that matter, not too many TV receivers.

The satellites will be able to relay programs from transmitters thousands of miles away directly to community television sets. Whether these community TV sets concentrate on cops-and-robbers programs and enlarge the image of the Ugly American or on programs that will help the viewers grow into their rightful place in this world depends, to a large degree, I submit, on whether those of you in education curse TV's darkness or light some ingenious candles.

Likewise, if you are innovative enough, videodiscs will make it possible for you to convert many of the TV sets in affluent societies into at least part-time classrooms.

To be sure, many videodiscs will be little more than updated soap operas. But I like to think of them as living books. Many books, perhaps most of them, have little real value. Yet, other books contain the works of Shakespeare and Shaw, the art of Rembrandt and Renoir, and the wisdom of Aristides and Aristotle, all of which videodiscs can also provide.

Of course, it is much easier to propose than to accomplish what I am suggesting. In fact, it probably sounds ridiculous to you, sort of an impossible dream.

But then, educators shouldn't be afraid to dream. Almost 70 years ago in Russia, Professor Boris Rosing first told me of his dream—electronically taking and transmitting live pictures through the air.

2.

Synopsis of Television in Education

Donald G. Perrin

Television has a greater impact on our day-to-day lives than any other medium. It plays a major role in determining the way we live, the way we communicate and the way we learn. Our living patterns have assumed television as a prime source of news, culture and entertainment. It becomes a baby sitter and tutor for the young, and a major contact with the outside world for the aged. It permeates urban and rural life with a bill of fare ranging from sales pitches to soap operas. With the advent of satellites, television programs can now be received at any point on the surface of the earth, and even by airplanes on trans-oceanic flights.

Our conversations, aspirations and activities are shaped by our television experiences but primarily by commercial television and educational (public) television. Instructional television is not competitive because of its limited budgets and audiences. Its expected impact on American education has been largely negated by poor acceptance by the school community as a whole— students, teachers and administrators. Students object to crude and unimaginative programs produced with shoe-string budgets. Their experience with commercial television establishes their

Donald G. Perrin is Chief, Instructional Technology Office, Secretary of Defense, Directorate for Audiovisual Activities, Office of Information for the Armed Forces. He is on leave from his position as Professor of Education, University of Maryland.

7

expectancy for interest level and production quality. Teachers object to synchronizing their schedules with TV, and often have pedagogical disagreements with the content and methodology. Administrators often do not understand either the potential or the logistics of televised instruction, and fail to provide the appropriate level of support. And so ITV, where it exists, tends to be inadequate. The most powerful communication medium in the history of civilization is, at best, under-utilized in our schools.

Instructional television has a tremendous potential. It can motivate, excite and involve large numbers of people of all ages. It can transport the viewer to any location in the past, present and future, in the realms of fact or fiction, reality or fantasy. It shares the most ideal viewing position with every viewer. It can make visible to all at the same time what would normally be visible only to one, such as the image from a microscope or a telescope. It can alternate close-up and distant views, using the zoom lens to make smooth transitions. Abstract concepts can be concretely visualized by animation. And videotape allows these experiences to be recorded and accessed at a later time, or replayed repeatedly, at normal or varied rates of playback speed, for analysis of an event. Television messages can be broadcast or transmitted along a wire. They are so available and so inexpensive (where the number of consumers is large) that television, whether for instruction or entertainment, can be used for single viewers or small groups.

In general, these potentials have not been realized for instructional television. The major products are, as Dr. Zworykin claims, not imaginative, innovative or exciting. They do not do the things which television is especially suited to do. Even after 25 years the major product of ITV is still the talking face, and not the infinite possibilities the talking face cannot be. Minimal economic resources and production skills have so limited ITV that many would say it is not yet a force to be reckoned with in American education.

There is a great deal of evidence to indicate that ETV is having a significant impact. The advent of public television is the single most significant factor. The success of "Sesame Street," "The Electric Company," and "Mr. Rogers Neighborhood," and the many network programs ("specials") on substantive issues is another. And the extensive offering of broadcast ETV programs in most major cities of the United States is an established fact of life. It is true that some schools still store TV equipment in the AV closet along with opaque, slide and film projectors. It is also true that some schools have installed TV sets in their classrooms, and have a master antenna system, studio, film-chain and videotape as possible program sources. The ease and versatility of videotape is the key to efficient use. Videotape is ideal for recording local events, for producing TV lessons or for storing programs for use at an instructionally appropriate time. But royalty and copyright problems have limited the tremendous economic advantage of re-using programs on videotape.

It would be unfair to make the copyright law the only villain. The present organization of the school systems and the traditional patterns of media use are major limiting factors. Markets as small as a single school system cannot afford to produce a product as technically polished as "Sesame Street" or the equivalent of a network "special." Also, so long as media, including TV, are selected and controlled by each individual teacher, TV will be limited to a minor or supporting role, or discarded entirely. Recent programs, such as the Clark "Civilisation" series or Bronowski's "Ascent of Man," have demonstrated the capability of TV to expand the curriculum and to reach toward the educational potentials of the medium. The producers of Continental Classroom and Sunrise Semester may well have dreamed of programs such as these. Continental Classroom, with its crude programs and early morning audiences, commanded a daily audience upwards of 250,000. The "Ascent of Man" will probably achieve a national audience of 25 million. The tradition initiated with Continental Classroom where students could enroll for credit in local schools and colleges has burgeoned to the level of the Open University which, in the British Isles, has permitted an academic degree to be completed via television. This concept has been modified and further refined in this country, as described by Jack McBride in his chapter in this book.

The professionalizing of ITV, where it has occurred, may be attributable in part to the fierce competition and polished production by the commercial broadcasters. A more significant factor is the development of networks, consortia and libraries to extend the audience, and thus reduce the cost per viewer. Los Angeles County found it more economical to produce one or two programs of excellent quality and exchange these for series produced by other school systems. National Education Television received grants from the National Science Foundation to do quality programs for national distribution. The Midwest Program for Airborne Television (MPATI) demonstrated the feasibility of production and broadcasting to serve a multi-state area from a single airborne transmitter. And the Great Plains Library has provided a source of TV program material to supplement local efforts, networks and consortia. Another excellent source of program material, educational films, has not been freely used because of the high royalties and difficulties in getting clearance for TV distribution.

Until recently ITV required proximity to a large population center, or the availability of suitable production facilities for closed circuit television. Community antenna (cable TV) systems have successfully opened up fringe areas except for those most remote, like parts of the Rocky Mountains and Appalachia. Airborne satellites are now being used for this purpose, and in Alaska two-way television is providing emergency services to remote areas. Adding the inter-continental satellites, the hardware potential for instructional transmission is virtually unlimited.

Roles of Instructional Television

Television has many instructional roles, the principal ones being total instruction; as a major resource; a supplemental resource; for enrichment; and for evaluation.

The research in both television and film as alternatives to traditional methods finds the media to be at least as effective as a good teacher in most instances. Thus total television instruction, where careful preparation and developmental testing substitute for student-teacher interaction, has already proven to be a viable alternative to traditional classroom instruction. There is other research which shows that television instruction is equally effective when conducted in alternate learning environments, in settings other than classrooms—in study areas, self-instructional laboratories, even at home and in dormitories.

Most educators and ITV producers would agree that television is most effective when combined with other learning experiences. This has been borne out by a large number of studies using television in conjunction with traditional instruction or with other media. The categories of television as a major resource and television as a supplemental resource belong here. The combined method or "package" is most effective when the separate elements are designed to work together. For instance, where the medium is the major resource, a human instructor might be used for motivation, introduction and follow-up. Where the medium is a supplemental resource, it might provide an overview, illustrations or summary. Learning is significantly better than traditional instruction when television serves as an integral component with other methods, techniques and media to comprise a *total learning system.*

Enrichment implies content and experiences beyond those required in the curriculum. For this reason, these experiences are not specific and not clearly defined in most instances. The research in incidental learning and secondary content seem most appropriate to this area. The lack of specificity suggests that the over-all learning would be less than for an equivalent experience focused on predetermined goals.

Television is used for self-evaluation in micro-teaching and in many diagnostic situations. Similarly, television may be used to present common experiences, either live or recorded, for group discussion and evaluation. There is abundant research to confirm the effectiveness of such use, with significant gains over conventional methods in many instances.

One finding which appears consistently throughout the research is a reduction in learning time compared to conventional methods. This can be attributed to the careful organization of the information, and the use of audio-visual methods of communication. Another finding which is sporadically reported is increased retention.

Television research parallels the research in film and other audio-visual media in its examination of group learning, comparison with alternative methods of instruction, correlation of learning with audience characteristics, and the effect of variables in production and use.

The findings seem to be very similar in each case; indeed, there appears to be little if any difference in learning from television and film if the two media are used the same way. The essential elements seem to be the interaction between content, audience and presentation factors. The particular medium (e.g., film, TV) or the means of transmission (cable, satellite) does not change the content. However, differences in learner preference and learner expectations of different media do produce measurable long-term effects in some instances. Also there are powerful cognitive effects, not by a particular medium per se considered as a whole (e.g., by television), but by the instructional use to which the particular attributes, comprising a given medium, are put.

Audience factors must be considered in the design and presentation of content. Motivation, relevance, pacing and vocabulary are crucial elements which must be correlated with media literacy, intelligence, formal education, age, sex, previous experience with the subject and predisposition toward the subject. The wide variety of formats from which the producer must choose comprises yet another dimension requiring resolution.

There have been many comparisons of program format to determine the effect of message design on learning. Contributing to the frequent no-significant-difference findings in research results is the fact that all too often programs, originally designed to serve other functions, have been subsequently pressed into service as research vehicles. Considering the many variables in design and presentation, the need for more tightly controlled research is evident.

The advent of computers and the research in programmed instruction have produced a new trend: relating content and presentation variables to the level and learning style of each individual student. In time, this will produce a more adequate theoretical base for designing ITV programs. Programmed instruction also emphasizes the concept of validation, where the responses of sample audiences are used for revision prior to final production. Film and TV are too expensive for repeated production and revision, so various short-cut approaches such as prototype production and pre-production testing have been devised to allow validation for a fractional increase in cost. Research on methods of pre-production testing has been going on for over two decades, but where ITV budgets are very small to begin with, this element is all too easily eliminated.

Improved methodology for research and evaluation has given added credibility to formative and summative evaluation as an integral part of the production procedure. (See the chapter by Williams and Stanford in this book.)

The present and future thrust seems to be toward matching personality factors (cognitive style), previous experience and presentation factors in a diagnostic-prescriptive manner. New research models to accommodate multiple variables with relatively small populations and experiment-specific programs may accelerate the production of usable research findings. In the interim, ITV will remain an art more than a science, dependent on creative and innovative communicators who enrich their art with the findings of research.

3.

Instructional Development
in Instructional Television

Diana R. Carl

Anyone working in instructional television (ITV) will testify to the high cost, time and multiple efforts involved in the production of an instructional program. Commercial television has ready access to funds to produce programs. Instructional television does not necessarily have these resources. One question of immediate concern to potential funders is whether a substantial investment in a proposed program will be justified. Ives (1971) pointed out the need to collect data on the results of educational media services which can show that those funds invested have been worthwhile. Mielke (1975a) stressed the futility of providing funds to initiate production of high-cost educational television only to suddenly withdraw them to support other projects. Clearly, a potential funder wants to insure that any investment made will show a likelihood of success. But in spite of this the amount of testing of educational programs for educational and economic effectiveness is limited (National Academy of Engineering, 1974).

Production efforts need to have accurate information in order to assure that the program is in line with its intended goals. Blakely (1974) and Himmelweit (1971) noted that a broadcaster is in danger of creating a program for a non-existent audience, and therefore is in need of accurate feedback to aid him in structuring

Diana R. Carl is a doctoral candidate in Instructional Systems Technology at Indiana University, Bloomington, and a consultant to the University of Mid-America and Memorial University of Newfoundland.

the program efforts. But Hall (1975) pointed out that while this is the ideal, production decisions are based more on intuitions than on factual data. The common notion in production is that researchers and evaluators are needed only after the program has been produced (Mielke, 1973). The assumption behind this is that any "well-produced" educational program will be effective (ACNO, 1975). But, as the Advisory Council points out, this is a false assumption. Program efforts should be preceded by planning with focus on the learners and the objectives to be realized. If the producer is to make rational decisions in an attempt to insure the effectiveness of the effort, he needs to have access to factual data and to be able to weigh this information in a systematic manner. The purpose of instructional development in ITV, therefore, is twofold: to create programming which is likely to be effective because it is based on a solid, rational approach, and secondly, to produce verifiable evidence of that success. It is the purpose of this chapter to define the extent of the presence of instructional development procedures used in ITV facilities described in the literature and for which the writer was able to obtain information. Although not all of the facilities examined deal exclusively in television, all share the commonality of being actively engaged in producing instructional television programs.

Instructional Development Models

A model is, simply, an approach. An instructional development model is an approach to designing instruction which its producer believes will aid him in identifying those elements which make up the instructional situation, and then aid the developers in their assimilation of an effective instructional package. The focus of a model can be based on the assumptions the designer holds about the learner, the subject matter or his philosophy in general. But more generally it appears as if those factors immediate to the design situation are more influential in determining the features of the model.

The benefit of a model seems to be that it provides a clear, systematic approach to designing instruction. The disadvantage appears to be a model's breakdown in generalization from one situation to the next.

Instructional development models differ greatly in their components. However, in terms of considerations which descriptions of models contain, several divisions can be drawn: needs assessment and goals generation, learner analysis (sometimes refered to as audience analysis), content identification, objective identification, strategizing (in the case of television the terms format and media selection appear more appropriate), and formative and summative evaluation. In Figure 1 these components are graphed as they appear to be taken into consideration in various ITV production facilities surveyed in this study.

Differences noted in the figure appear to be related to the extent of service, i.e., facilities serving one immediate institution or area or those servicing more than one institution or area, and to the monetary, material and human resources available to the facility for the effort. In some instances it was difficult to classify some programming as truly instructional in nature. The discussion of ETV/ITV differences will not be undertaken here for the purpose of clarity. However, the feeling was that if the program, whether intended for viewing in school or at home, appeared to have some *instructional intent*, it warranted attention in this study. It does not include the occasional instructional endeavors of commercial broadcasters.

The definition of instructional development trends in ITV is hazy at best. The checks in the columns appear if the sources consulted expressed an action or concern for the factor. It is important to point out that three problems may exist in the graph. First, this may not be representative of ITV in general. The fact that the agencies studied were generally already published in itself says that they may be different from similar operations in some aspects of development. Secondly, the terminology was not consistent. At times the writer sensed that, while not being discussed explicitly, the underlying meaning of some practices

Figure 1a

Agency or Project	Needs and Goals		Audience Identification			Objective Specification			Content Specification	
	Needs Assessment	Goal Formation	Demographics	Entry Behavior	Program Preference	Learner Based	Content Based	Stated in Evaluative Terms	Task Analysis	Entry Behavior Specified
Agency for Instructional Television (AIT)	✓	✓	✓	✓	✓	✓	✓		✓	✓
Appalachia Educational Laboratory (AEL) for National Effort in Reading	✓	✓	✓		✓	✓	✓			
Adult Learning Program Service (Project Strive)	✓	✓	✓			✓	✓	✓	✓	✓
British Open University										
Carpenter's (1969) Survey of ITV in Music Education										
Cavert's (1972) ITV Study									✓	
Center for Innovation in Teaching the Handicapped	✓	✓								
Chicago TV College	✓	✓	✓	✓	✓	✓	✓	✓	✓	✓
Children's Television Workshop (CTW)	✓	✓	✓		✓	✓	✓		✓	✓
Dual Audio Television			✓	✓	✓	✓		✓		✓
Far West Educational Laboratory	✓	✓								
Indiana University ITV Service										
Joyce: TV and Social Studies	✓	✓					✓			
Maine Viewer-Active Series	✓	✓					✓	✓		
Mississippi Authority for ETV	✓	✓		✓		✓	✓			
Ohio State Dept. of Ed. ITV Div.	✓	✓	✓	✓	✓	✓	✓			
Southwest Educational Laboratory	✓	✓	✓	✓		✓	✓			
State University of Neb. (SUN)	✓	✓	✓	✓	✓	✓	✓		✓	✓
TICCIT: Brigham Young Univ.	✓	✓					✓		✓	✓
Univ. of Wisconsin (RFD)									✓	✓
Webster College						✓			✓	✓

Figure 1b

Agency or Program	Format and Media Selection				Formative Evaluation				Summative Evaluation			
	Based on Content Specs.	Based on Audience Specs.	Based on Goals and Objectives	Suppl. Media Considered	Implemented	Use of Expert Opinion	Use of Audience Appeal Data	Use of Objective Attainment Data	Implemented	Use of Objective Attainment Data	Use of Audience Appeal Data	Use of External Evaluators
Agency for Instructional Television (AIT)	✓	✓	✓	✓	✓	✓	✓	✓				
Appalachia Educational Laboratory (AEL) for National Effort in Reading			✓	✓	✓				✓			
Adult Learning Program Service (Project Strive)		✓	✓					✓	✓			
British Open University	✓		✓	✓	✓	✓						
Carpenter's (1969) Survey of ITV in Music Education												
Cavert's (1972) ITV Study	✓											
Center for Innovation in Teaching the Handicapped	✓	✓	✓	✓	✓			✓	✓			
Chicago TV College		✓	✓	✓	✓		✓	✓	✓	✓	✓	✓
Children's Television Workshop (CTW)	✓	✓	✓		✓	✓	✓	✓	✓	✓	✓	✓
Dual Audio Television		✓	✓		✓		✓	✓	✓	✓	✓	
Far West Educational Laboratory			✓									
Indiana University ITV Service			✓	✓								
Joyce: TV and Social Studies	✓		✓	✓	✓		✓	✓				✓
Maine Viewer-Active Series	✓		✓		✓							
Mississippi Authority for ETV	✓	✓	✓	✓				✓	✓		✓	
Ohio State Dept. of Ed. ITV Div.		✓	✓									
Southwest Educational Laboratory			✓									
State University of Neb. (SUN)	✓	✓	✓	✓	✓		✓	✓	✓	✓	✓	✓
TICCIT: Brigham Young Univ.	✓	✓	✓		✓	✓	✓		✓	✓	✓	
Univ. of Wisconsin (RFD)	✓		✓		✓				✓			
Webster College	✓	✓	✓		✓						✓	

observed seemed to be congruent with those factors of concern to developers. Therefore, some data are based on inference. A third problem arose in determining the levels within each factor. Most of these were determined through reading the literature in instructional development and then selecting those factors which appeared to apply to the problem at hand. Therefore, the categories selected may not be as clear-cut as the graph represents them. Realizing the limitations of the study, the following trends appear to be discernible:

1. Those ITV facilities which appear to have more resources and serve larger areas seem to share many of the same elements of the instructional development process, including a concern for assessing needs, specifying the audience and objectives, selection of format and a recognition of the need to formatively evaluate a program.

2. In smaller ITV facilities, with fewer resources, content appears to determine format; in larger ITV facilities, with more resources, audience findings appear to be the main determinant of format.

3. The concern for systematic evaluation appears to be greater in larger ITV facilities than in smaller ones.

4. Facilities engaged in producing programs for at-home viewing appear to be concerned mainly with audience identification and analysis.

5. Facilities engaged in producing programs for in-school viewing appear to be concerned mainly with content identification and analysis.

Goals and Objectives

If one intends to produce an instructional television program, there is an underlying assumption, either tacit or explicit, that the producer expects the viewer to come away with something: to know, to appreciate or to do something. Tyler (1973) realized that these kinds of expected reactions, whether they are covert or overt, are actually patterns of behavior which the teacher or producer expects the viewer to acquire. If he recognizes this expectation, the producer can gain more control over the design of his program, but if he DEFINES it more explicitly he gains even more direction in shaping the experience. The responsible ITV producer scrutinizes the objectives, and he structures them to be more consistent with other factors in the program's context (Lumsdaine, 1972). Tyler (1971) said there are five factors in the selection of objectives: the culture in which the viewer operates, the behavioral status of the viewer, the subject matter knowledge, the relevance of the objectives to other objectives (this also includes noting conflicts in objectives) and consistency with learning theory (e.g., can the objective be realisitically taught, and through what methods will they be learned most effectively?). In addition, Briggs (1970) suggests the usefulness of developing a "tree of objectives" for the program so that the main objective can be examined in terms of its enabling sub-objectives. The program can then be structured accordingly.

[While most ITV producers expressed an interest in formulating objectives, the most thorough scrutiny and systematic formulation was evidenced in the efforts of the Children's Television Workshop (CTW), Appalachia Educational Laboratory (AEL), State University of Nebraska (SUN), Agency for Instructional Television (AIT), Southwestern Educational Laboratory and the Far West Educational Laboratory—the large producers of instructional television.]One very persistent problem even in these was the formulation of objectives which were consistent with the goals of the producing facility and those perceived as being the goals of the intended audience, education and U.S. society. For example, the mission of public television according to Millard (1974) is to attempt "to serve a series of specialized audiences with programming each needs most and loves best." One can begin to see the problems of defining "needs and loves" and "specialized audiences." The problem of justifying program objectives in terms of this goal raises questions about what is a true need and want and for whom. In the view of some individuals, the objectives of the program could be consistent with these goals, while others would argue that the needs and wants have been contrived. This has especially been the case in public affairs programming (Brown, 1972; Leonard, 1974; U.S. Senate, 1974).

While the presence of behavioral objectives permeates ITV, it is questionable whether the assessment of conditions of the learner and the environment in which the new behavior is to occur is adequate. Little evidence was found to support a conclusion that such an assessment takes place, outside of some larger facilities which appear to be the exceptions. At the same time there seems to be a concern on the part of producers to create programs which can be used by more than one audience or for more than one purpose, possibly due to the expense of production (Brown, 1975; Lesser, 1974; Perry and LaBarr, 1975; Thiagarajan, 1975). Rather than assessing the conditions for which the program will be used, the producers first ask how many and what types of audiences and what purposes the program can be structured to serve, and then, how the objectives of the potential program can be modified to include these new factors. Grayson (1972) pointed out the use of this technique in creating more effective programs for the cost involved. Thiagarajan (1975) expressed the worth of this strategy from the point of view of restructuring objectives as the testing of a program indicates resulting behaviors not explicitly stated in the objectives. Two advantages to this approach are evident. First, considering the time and research which are put into program formation, should unexpected benefits be observed or the potential audience expanded, the cost-effectiveness is increased. Secondly, if a program fails to meet the expectations for which it was intended, the realization and sensitivity to unintended results can aid in restructuring the program, the objectives or the conditions under which the objectives are to be attained.

In larger broadcast facilities such as CTW the identification of learners has been more influential than any other concern in defining objectives. This may be a function of the role of public television in serving specialized audiences. Audience demographics and entry behaviors are probably the most researched factors in the development of instructional programs seen on public television.]

In addition to being flexible, the objectives must be realistic. Cavert (1974) recognized that television cannot be expected to change a universe. It is unrealistic to expect one instructional program or series to result in long term behavioral changes—especially for changing behaviors which are deeply engrained. If such change is wanted, a producer must think in terms of stimuli he can provide outside of the confines of the program but within the viewer's environment to provide the extra incentive to behavioral change which the program is not able to present. Again, this challenges the producer to systematically analyze the goals and objectives of the program in terms of its components and the existing behavior patterns of the target audience.

Perhaps "Sesame Street" with its more cognitive objectives and younger audience was more effective because the objectives were more immediately attainable during the viewing of the program (Lesser, 1974). "Feeling Good" is another story. The goal of illness prevention and health care behavioral changes directed at young parents—especially those in lower socioeconomic groups—may have been too broad and subject to too many extra-program variables to be as effective as producers would have liked. Had the problems of changing such established behavioral patterns been acknowledged, CTW personnel would have recognized that a reassessment of the program objectives to make them more consistent with established learning theory might be in order.

In instructional television intended for in-school use, explicitly stated objectives appear abundant. But in terms of relating the objectives in the program to content and to the social environment in which the student functions, perhaps more scrutiny is needed. Tyler (1973) pointed out that behavioral objectives are only of value when they help the instruction to attain the goals for which it is intended.

Audience Analysis

The learner as the center of attention in designing instruction is widely acknowledged (Briggs, 1970; Merrill, 1971; Popham, 1970; Stowe and Schwen, 1973; Tyler, 1971). However, the degree of focus on the learner varies greatly. In mass media the goal has generally been to aim a program at the maximum possible number of people in order to gain a large audience share. But Adams (1971) and Millard (1974) point out that audience potential is secondary to the potential of an *instructional* program to fill certain needs and wants of smaller "specialized audiences." It is at this point in public broadcasting that the problem of learner analysis becomes audience analysis, and possibly, due to conflicting ideas of what the goals of public broadcasting and education are, becomes confounded.

The assumption producers hold that television programs are good only if they attract viewers has led to a tendency in public television to gather data which will provide evidence of the appeal of a program rather than of its instructional effectiveness (Sequin *et al.* 1974). An evaluator for "Feeling Good" stated that he and other evaluators were under pressure from producers to evaluate the appeal of the program much more than its instructional effectiveness.

True learner analysis is not ignored in some development situations. Bretz (1971), Lesser (1974) and Loasa (1974) reported that learner analysis both for designing the program and for diffusion of it were practiced for "Sesame Street" and for "Carrascolendas." Cavert (1974) listed many factors bearing a direct relationship to the viewer's potential to watch and learn which must be considered in designing an instructional program. The problem appears to be that for instructional television intended for at-home viewing, producers have been unable to decide whether the programs (1) should be designed to attract an audience, or (2) to provide optimum instruction. The push to attract viewers seems to be short-changing the need to design instructionally effective programs. Perhaps a concentrated effort to identify the distinction between *learner analysis* for designing the instruction and *audience analysis* for optimum diffusion and implementation of the program is warranted if the efforts for diffusion are not to be counter-productive to the original intents of the instructional program. As the situation exists, instructional effectiveness appears to be sacrificed to gain a larger audience. While not entirely a solution in itself, the realization of two distinct types of learner analysis based on different intents (learning outcomes and diffusion) may lead more clearly to the gathering of data on learners and to the possible application of the data to program design and diffusion efforts, so that the maximum share possible in a specialized audience will be exposed to the program and will receive optimum instruction.

The types of measures used to collect data about the learner are standard in only a few respects. Audience demographics such as age, ethnicity, frequency of viewing, program preference, occupation, head of household, family size and socioeconomic status are common. Other measures, such as entry behavior, relation of socioeconomic status to preferred program format, etc., vary greatly with the program efforts. Most of these analyses appear to be constructed and conducted specifically for the program being researched and perhaps due to this have questionable reliability and validity.

Learner analysis appears to be stressed to a lesser degree in in-school instructional television, for several reasons. First, the audience may remain basically unchanged in developing many programs, making extensive observation unnecessary for each new program development (Thiagarajan, 1975). Secondly, the more subject-centered role of program development in relation to the established curriculum of the institution places more emphasis on content development based on an instructor's view of the content and his own knowledge of his students (Perry and LaBarr, 1975). Thirdly, the motivation to watch may be there before the student views the program. Therefore, the need to discover what appeals to the learner may be of secondary importance. Molenda (1974) and Bretz (1971) noted the effect of internal motivation on a student's desire to learn from instructional television. Cavert (1972) and Carpenter (1969) in their studies revealed, however, that in most of the ITV facilities surveyed, learner analysis takes the form of mere cursory observation.

Content Analysis

One of the unfortunate assumptions which appears to characterize instructional development efforts in far too many ITV facilities is that the content of a program is "self-evident." Likewise, it is said that there is no need for delving into such things as "enabling objectives," sequencing, problems in content discrimination or generalization. The role of task or content analysis seems to be interpreted differently at times: i.e., should the task be fitted to the learner or the learner to the task? While the development effort is justifiably focused on the learner and his components (Merrill, 1971), acknowledgment of the multi-component nature of content can provide the developer with insights into designing optimal instruction (Gagne, 1971). Schramm (1972) said, "If the goal is learning, then the content elements of an ITV program must be selected and used so as to contribute to the specifically desired learning." Yet in only four of the cases surveyed did content analysis seem to be stressed: at the Center for Innovation in Teaching the Handicapped (Thiagarajan, 1975), in CTW's efforts for "Sesame Street" (Lesser, 1974), at the British Open University (Dorn, 1974; Kitzens and Knot, 1972) and at AIT (Brown, 1975).

Although not normally practiced as a systematic and rational effort, the notion of content analysis appears to be of greater concern to smaller ITV facilities which serve a relatively fixed audience as described in the previous section. Cavert (1972) stated that content appropriateness was the basis for designing programs in 95 percent of the ITV facilities he surveyed. In some cases the trend seems to be to leave the content and program design to the teachers doing the program or to content experts rather than to subject it to the process of development. This is the policy at Chicago TV College (Bretz, 1971), at Indiana University Instructional Television Service (Perry and LaBarr, 1975) and at varied ITV facilities in the U.S. as noted by Cavert (1972) and Carpenter (1969). A model used by the Mississippi Authority for Educational TV stresses content analysis by screening the potential script through several curriculum committees and content consultants (Welliver, 1972).

[In the example from "Sesame Street" (Lesser, 1974) the analysis of the types of tasks the child was expected to engage in appeared to be based on the behavioral categories described by Gagne (1971). Cavert explained another approach to task analysis based on different levels and types of objectives and Piaget's developmental stages (Cavert, 1974).]

Clearly, the realization of a logic characterizing a given content and the appropriate use of this logic in facilitating learning is not yet part of the design and development process in most of ITV. The need to "aim" a program at a target audience has led producers to concentrate on the audience. But if the audience is to really *learn* from the program, the content must be broken down into component parts which are meaningfully related. The designer must create a situation in which the component parts add up to a whole which is greater than the sum of its parts, so that the learner—after experiencing it—understands the body of knowledge and can *use* it.

Media Selection, Program Format and Production

The notion of selecting the media after objectives have been selected, and learners and content identified, is found readily in design and development literature (Briggs, 1970; Davies, 1973; Tosti and Ball, 1969, for example). But Hawkridge (1973) and Thiagarajan (1975) have noted that media selection is determined in many cases *before* the program is conceived. In some cases it is the only available means; in others the investment in hardware will lead to pressure on developers to design instruction which assures the hardware will be used. In still others the nature of the learning experience or audience preempts the decision to use alternative media.

Of course, in facilities specializing in televised instruction, the medium is predetermined. The use of television as the primary medium of instruction in this case has immediate relevance to the goals of the facility. Although not specifically tackled in the literature nor discussed by those interviewed, the sources implied a trend toward the use of supplemental materials in conjunction with the television program. In 1974 CTW established a product division (CTW, 1975). One reason given for this move was the reinforcing potential these materials might have for the program, which could add to the program's effectiveness. But a more important reason for considering the use of other media even though television serves as the primary medium is related to the objectives themselves. The concern for just what the medium of television alone *can* do to change behavior is being felt. Ulrich of Western Michigan University questioned the ability of "Sesame Street" to change behavior (Lesser, 1974). Of course, many evaluation efforts undertaken by both CTW and independent forces have indicated that this is not necessarily so. Rather than grouping all behavioral objectives together into one category, it may be better to ask "what are the *types* of objectives television is capable of achieving?" and "what are the long range behavioral changes which television can be reasonably expected to produce?" It is fairly evident that these two questions contain a host of others which warrant attention. The point here is that developers should *not* close the door to the use of other media when evidence exists that television or mass media channels may not produce the desired changes.

A case in point is the program "Feeling Good." According to CTW the goals of the program were to provide adult viewers "with authoritative health information and motivate them toward better health habits" (CTW, 1975). As stated, the goals appear no less likely to be achieved than the goals of "Sesame Street." But in the formative evaluation efforts described by program evaluators, it would appear as if the outcomes actually wanted were much more extensive than the stated goals. Mielke (1975b) explained that one outcome seen as an important measure of expected behavioral change was an increased number of visits to a doctor or clinic. Another was a change in the food purchasing habits to be more consistent with a healthy diet. The results obtained showed no difference between those viewing the program and those not viewing it (Mielke, 1975b). Yet the evaluators expected there to be significant differences between these groups. Reason *not* to expect this change to occur, however, had previously been presented by Rogers and Shoemaker in a discussion of mass media and interpersonal communication channels. They identified mass media channels as being more effective in the diffusion of information and less effective in persuading persons to *change* their behavior. Interpersonal channels are more effective in the persuasion function (Rogers and Shoemaker, 1971). Carlson (1974) and Niemi (1971) also expressed this same idea. The decision to use mass media exclusively in attempting to make changes in established behaviors needs to be based on more than the fact that the primary role of the agency is concerned with the production of television programs. AIT appears to have taken this into consideration in the design of programming. The use of an open-ended format in some series necessitates the use of another medium: that of group discussion (AIT, 1974; Brown, 1975). In the case of "Feeling Good," however, the use of supplementary media did not appear to be actively considered in the formative efforts. Funds were distributed to local stations to establish outreach projects, but the use of funds and the design of these projects were left to the discretion of the local stations (CTW, 1975). In the design of the program itself no formative evaluation was conducted to determine which combinations of the program and interpersonal strategies would be most effective in producing behavioral changes (Webster, 1975).

The problem is that the actual limitations of television as a vehicle for behavioral change are not yet clarified. The need to identify the types of objectives for which television alone will suffice and the types for which television in combination with other channels will be more effective appears to warrant much more exploration.

Likewise, television formats for realizing certain types of objectives need more research. Format selection is that portion of the design process in which the products of the previous decision-making on goals, audience and content begin to take on the characteristics of a program entity. Traditionally in broadcast television the selection of format, the design of the script, selection of props, etc., are the domain of production. But if the *total* program effort is to be successful, the inputs from the prior analyses must be actively considered in the format design and in other parts of the production effort. For example, Di Vesta (1971) noted the need to match instructional strategies to individual differences in creating an effective instructional system. This cues ITV developers to the intimate relationship of format selection to audience preferences. Popham (1970) suggests that the learning atmosphere be warm, supporting, satisfying: suggestions which might explain the success of "Mister Rogers Neighborhood."

Lesser (1972) noted the need to combine content with format so that more effective learning can occur. That research efforts *were* present in the production considerations for "Sesame Street" is the main thesis of Lesser's book (Lesser, 1974). One means through which the research and production staffs were able to accomplish this was through the development of a "Writers Manual" which served as a guide for scripting programs and selecting specific stimuli. Designers at AIT do this anew for each program (Brown, 1975). Once the goals, audience and content are firm, AIT designers write a "treatment": a story line or possible approach which could serve as the vehicle for presentation. It acts as a communication device from designers to writers to explain more clearly the intent of the program. Appearances suggest that this technique is effective. Through the use of the two devices described above it seems that the tendency to view content as "self-evident" in scripting is overcome.

Format based on intuition is common in ITV. The format used for "The Advocates" was based on court experiences (Bretz, 1971). Herd's description of efforts to produce "commercials that instruct" implies that format was arrived at intuitively (Herd, 1973). Dudek (1972) suggests that the need to view the selection of format and stimuli more systematically is important, yet he seems caught by a need to *entertain* at the expense of *instruction*. His assumption appears to be that format should be structured to catch and hold an audience much more than it should be designed to instruct per se. Good producers trust their instincts in producing entertaining programs. But is this a license to compromise instruction?

Intuition and instincts provide the flair and style which make an instructional television program stand out. To banish them from the program effort might be likened to removing the bouquet from a fine brandy. It is this intuitive gamble which sets the program apart from others with similar intents. But the failure to include those factors determined by the preceding design efforts can lead to programs based on a reality which exists only in the producer's mind. The selection of format is necessarily based on the design efforts.

While comparatively few, efforts in the systematic determination of format and stimuli do exist, mainly in larger ITV facilities. CTW efforts of "Sesame Street," Maine Educational Television, SUN and AIT have exemplified the logical fluidity of design and development into production.

Producers may be guilty of under-utilizing research in preparing format and stimulus materials, but researchers may also be guilty of not being familiar with the capabilities of the medium with which they are working. Lundgren (1972) noted that a good instructional television program makes use of the unique capabilities of the television medium. This is a challenge to designers to be intimately familiar with the unique properties, horizons and limitations of television so that they can engage in more meaningful developmental activity.

The basic assumption broadcast producers seem to hold at this crossroad in the design-production effort is that research is counter-creative: that the real success of a program lies in the creativity exhibited by the producer and writers in their attempt to create an entertaining and informational program. What appears to be unrealized is that finding out what gives pleasure to a person and how learning can be accomplished easiest and in ways which makes the experience enjoyable are among the primary concerns of the researchers with whom they work. If developmental efforts are ever to be used fluidly in production efforts, producers must acknowledge that the undertakings of developers are not in conflict with the intents of the producer. Likewise, developers must understand and appreciate the capabilities, limitations and production pressures the producer knows only too well.

Evaluation

A developer can design programs which he believes will be effective for the defined goals; but unless there is some feedback mechanism to let him know how in reality it is working, there is no way to either structure the design to better meet the goals of the program or to ascertain whether the completed program has been effective. This is the role of evaluation. It is the collection of objective evidence from groups representative of those for whom the program is intended (Weiss, 1972). This evidence is weighed against the criteria against which the program was set. Most simply stated, evaluation is the measurement of the outcomes of a program in reference to its intended goals. The purpose of an evaluation is to aid the developer and producer in making decisions about the program.

In the survey it was rare that the writer found little or no concern for feedback. However, the degree of precision of

evaluation varied greatly. Larger ITV with more resources undertook systematic evaluation efforts and utilized the results in
decision-making (AIT, 1974; Brown, 1975; CTW, 1975; Flaugher,
1974; Lesser, 1974; Loasa, 1974; Low, 1973; Shively, 1973). In
most other ITV units the concern for systematic evaluation is
rarely systematic or empirical. In a series of case studies of
institutions producing ITV programs for music education, Carpenter (1969) found that the concern for evaluation of locally
produced programs was lacking. While a general concern for
feedback on effectiveness was noted, feedback consisted of
opinions of teachers using the programs and frequency-of-use data
gathered through cursory and unrigorous methods. Cavert (1972)
in a survey of instructional television service in the U.S. noted this
same type of loose, generally unreliable evaluation.

Weiss (1972) and many others distinguish between formative
and summative evaluation. Formative evaluation is fed back into
the development of a program and is used in improving it, while
summative evaluation measures the outcomes of a finished
program against its goals. In most units expressing a concern for
systematic evaluation, both types were practiced. Brown (1975)
and Thiagarajan (1975) indicated that AIT and CITH engaged in
only formative evaluation under normal circumstances.

The extent of engagement in either type of evaluation seems
to be related to the funds and time available for evaluation. Low
(1973) stated that the time limitations placed on developers make
them slip through evaluation efforts rather unrigorously. Loasa
(1974) stated that rigor and replicability belong in formative
evaluation and should not be short-changed. Rigorous methodology and replicability of a formative effort would satisfy the need
to contribute to the body of existing scientific knowledge while
also satisfying the immediate needs of the producers (Loasa,
1974). The concern for adequate funding of evaluation (Weiss,
1972; Wholey, 1975) would tend to lend some support to the
argument for formative efforts designed to suit this dual purpose.
The Advisory Council of National Organizations (1975) concurred

on the need for research which could be used in making policy and design decisions in a variety of ITV situations. Coleman (1971) described a model based on the use of pre-existing research as a basis for decision-making on program design.

At CTW, AIT and AEL it is standard procedure to bring in evaluators at the onset of the design effort. This is the exception rather than the rule. Mielke (1973) noted that it is quite common for researchers and evaluators not to be brought in until after the program has been completed. Such action, however, preempts the decision to formatively evaluate, and, moreover, deprives the evaluators of information they should have in order to adequately evaluate a program. Yet even in some efforts in which instructional development procedures were employed, the need for including evaluation from the initiation of the design was overlooked. Cavert (1974), unfortunately, did not express any due concern for evaluation to be present in the program from the beginning. Other less notable examples were easily found (e.g., Carpenter, 1969; Cavert, 1972; Gillom and Zimmer, 1972; Herd, 1973; Perry and LaBarr, 1975). Summative evaluation is the most commonly accepted form of evaluation noted in the literature. While undertaken, the measures are not always formulated with the goals of the program and the generating system. Seibert (1972) noted that evaluation methods used in educational broadcasting usually bear little if any relationship to the goals which the program is intended to reach. Referring to the tendency for ITV evaluations to be based solely on teacher opinions and frequency of use (Carpenter, 1969; Cavert, 1972), it is very difficult to justify the use of such "measures" as being criteria for the goals of the program, unless the goals were to change teacher opinions and frequency of use. Adams (1971) noted the need for evaluation efforts in public television to be more consistent with their own purposes than with those of commercial broadcasting. Audience ratings should be included only when audience potential is one of the objectives of the program. But by no means is audience potential for *any* ITV program the only criterion against which the program ought to be measured.

Measures to test the effectiveness of programs can be multiple (e.g., CTW, AIT, AEL, Southwestern Educational Laboratory and Far West Educational Laboratory) and test both learning and attitude toward viewing the program. Weiss (1972) has pointed out the need for measures to be flexible to allow for changes in the program and audience. It was difficult to ascertain whether such flexibility was truly present in many efforts examined. The efforts described at AIT by Brown (1975) appeared very flexible. Thiagarajan (1975) stated that all evaluation measures employed for both televised and other instruction produced at CITH are structured to take into account unintended outcomes of the programs.

Another concern of agencies engaging in systematic evaluation efforts is whether the evaluation should be conducted by an in-house or an external group. Weiss (1972) stated that both have advantages and disadvantages. In-house teams understand the workings of the program, their results are more likely to be used since producers have more confidence in the evaluators, and mistakes uncovered can be "kept in the family." Outside evaluators, on the other hand, can be more objective in their analyses; due to their detachment from the producing agency, they are more likely to gain public confidence; and they are able to remain autonomous. But in spite of these advantages they may lack the confidence of the program administrators or understanding of the program and its goals. Moreover, they may not be able to insure the use of their results. Weiss (1972) and Mielke (1973) recommend the use of in-house evaluation teams for formative evaluation efforts and the use of external teams for summative evaluation. The reasoning behind this is easily derived from the above statements.

The use of an external evaluating team may be related to the question of monetary funds available. It appears that those agencies with limited funds rely more on in-house efforts. CTW uses in-house teams in formative evaluation and an external team for summative evaluation (CTW, 1975; Lesser, 1974) as do AEL

(Shively, 1973), University of Wisconsin for "RFD" (McElreath, 1974), Southwestern Educational Laboratory (Loasa, 1974) and AIT (Brown, 1975). However, on the "Bread and Butterflies" project, AIT used an external team in formative efforts (Flaugher, 1974). Although it could not be determined whether external or internal teams were used in evaluations, both formative and summative evaluation were done for several productions described (Hood and Johnson, 1969; Low, 1973; Van De Bogart, 1972).

Cost-effectiveness

Cost-effectiveness is another concern of ITV evaluation. The federal government, a large source of funding for ITV, has shown a concern for results demonstrating that investments in programming yield maximum effectiveness and benefits (National Academy of Engineering, 1974; Rivlin, 1971; Wholey, 1975).

Indeed, cost-effectiveness seems to figure very prominently in evaluation and in everything done on broadcast television (Grayson, 1972; Lesser, 1974; Mielke, 1975a). Weiss (1972) stated that program benefits are difficult to quantify in order to obtain some kind of evaluative evidence on what kinds of and how much benefit have resulted from a program. While the "what kinds" are more easily interpreted in the specification of objectives, the "how much" can create problems: perhaps because in broadcast television the "how much" has been interpreted as size of audience more than as "how much of the benefit." In mass media channels it appears that cost-effectiveness has emphasized the size of the audience above the attainment of objectives. Perry (1975) at Indiana University Instructional Television Service explained how, when designing a program, he must justify the cost in terms of the number of campuses and students for which the program can be used. The point is that the relationship between mass media channels and cost-effectiveness may be influencing the design of programs much more than it ought to affect it. It is important to remember that for public television, for instance, the goal is *not* to attract as large an audience as possible (Millard, 1974). Therefore, cost-effectiveness analysis must necessarily take into consideration not the audience share relative to the size of all potential audiences within a viewing area, but rather the audience share relative to the predicted size of the specific target audience which is supposed to gain from viewing the program.

Producers trained in commercial broadcasting may be carrying over to public broadcasting some of the assumptions of cost-effectiveness which apply to commercial television, one of which is the need to attract a large audience share from the general audience in the viewing area. This may account for the push they seem to exercise in designing an instructional program to attract a large audience. Likewise, funders may be anxious to back a "hit" ITV program and tend to be more conscious of the ratings than of learning outcomes. If instructional television is to be successful, a distinction between mass audience and a specific target audience needs to be clarified to funders, administrators and producers in order to create an awareness that the attraction of a mass audience is not the primary nor the only goal of televised instruction. More emphasis should be placed on the quality of the experience provided. The mass-audience preoccupation of cost-effectiveness appears to have an effect on other uses of ITV. The notion of television as a *mass* medium has tended to be more predominant than other potential advantages of television, such as the ability to present an event to students while it is occurring at great distances or under conditions which make it impossible or inadvisable to allow students to experience the event directly. A traditional cost-effectiveness analysis under such circumstances could be highly misleading. Cost-effectiveness as an evaluative tool can provide excellent feedback on the investment made in an ITV program, but considering the meanings construed for cost-effectiveness in mass media and their repercussions for the design process, it is imperative that the meaning of cost-effectiveness for ITV be well-defined so that it does not interfere with the original goals of any ITV program.

Organizational and Interpersonal
Relationships

Models appear efficient on paper. But the procedures prescribed by a model are conducted by people: people who are subject to their own perceptions, interpersonal relationships and biases. No model can proceed successfully if the human components do not allow it to do so. Therefore, in an article examining the uses of instructional development techniques in ITV it is highly appropriate that the relationships between the human components be examined for the purpose of determining if there are any categories of personnel in the process between whom a lack of willingness to cooperate is evident. As in the design and development processes in other media, there appears to be a schism of potential magnitude between designers and producers of ITV programs. Although evidence to support this conclusion was not explicitly found, it is suspected that this is a problem more typical of larger broadcast agencies in which personnel divisions are more distinct than of smaller agencies in which several functions are undertaken by one person. Lesser (1972, 1974), Bretz (1971), Palmer (1972) and others attributed the success of "Sesame Street" to the efforts of producers and researchers to work together. The effort did not come easily. Researchers and producers both expressed doubts about the perceptions of the other.

Depending on the model referred to, one will find a model in which the design is accomplished by developers then turned over to production to become a product; a model in which this linearity is maintained but with developers serving as formative sources of information from which the producers can draw if they so choose; and a model in which all forces are engaged actively in all aspects of program synthesis from conception to final education—a truly cybernetic model. The CTW model, while appearing to fall under the last heading, has most recently shown signs that it bears more resemblance to models such as those in the second. Lesser (1974) and others have noted that in the production phase the decision to use or ignore the data from the design and development was strictly at the discretion of the producer. An evaluator for "Feeling Good" also noted that the producer was not always held accountable for his decisions. In this instance, research rather than serving a developmental function becomes a resource used only to support existing beliefs of the decision-making producers or to provide supporting evidence for decisions based on intuition. Hall (1975) noted that while the ideal is for producers to depend greatly on research in making decisions, in reality research is used only to reinforce previously formed beliefs and decisions. He also pointed out the suspicion of management for research findings in making decisions. The high degree of mistrust for research which CTW attempted to ease is apparently alive and seemingly as hostile as ever in 1976.

Why does it exist? There seem to be several factors which contribute to the friction. First, broadcast producers seem to hold the assumption that their main purpose in creating ITV programs is to attract as large an audience as possible (Lundgren, 1972). But instructional broadcasting, having different goals than commerical broadcasting, does not need to compete for an audience in most of its programming.

Secondly, there are the biases of producers that research efforts will somehow stifle the creative efforts which make a program unique (Seibert, 1972). As stated previously, the need to recognize that research used will not lead to a dull-dry program and that research provides the producer with an approximation of the true reality for which the program is being produced both need to be better understood.

Language differences lead to suspicion. Lesser (1974) pointed out the frustration of producers in attempting to understand the language of researchers. Himmelweit (1971) also noted a need for a common language so that researchers can provide the producer with the results of their analyses in a manner which facilitates the use of these results.

Fourthly, producers are willing to trust their own instincts much more than they are willing to trust research as a basis for decision-making. Yet AIT producers have been able to produce excellent instructional television using the information obtained in development (Brown, 1975). Perhaps this has to do with the position of the decision-making personnel relative to the production. Brown referred to it as "participatory development" in which all parties hash out differences on equal footing. When differences could not be resolved the consultants, who are normally in the effort from the onset, exercise authority in deciding the course of action.

But producers in most agencies *are* the decision-makers (Bretz, 1971; Lesser, 1974). Their training is production-oriented. In a review of an AEL pilot for "Around the Bend" (Shively, 1973), differences in perceptions of the program by ITV personnel and educational specialists were evident. One suggestion for closing this gap between developers and producers was proposed by Katzman, who suggested that university broadcast training programs add courses on "the sensible utilization of telecommunication research" data in order to teach new producers and administrators how to go about using research data in decision-making (Hall, 1975).

Researchers, on the other hand, may not be aware of the peculiar problems and pressures under which producers operate. Research findings are difficult to communicate to a producer working under time and production pressures (Ives, 1971). Lundgren (1972) said that a good ITV program makes use of the unique possibilities of the medium. Dorn (1974) said that BBC producers in Great Britain are expected to be experts on the subject on which the program is being produced for the Open University; but that faculty, the developers for the courses, are not required to be familiar with educational television. He questions their ability to make the most of the medium under the circumstances.

It appears that the researcher/producer relationship is a two-way street. If successful programming is to be produced and implemented, each must come more than half way. Even a small amount of familiarity with the practices, constraints and advantages each segment has to work with may be enough to create a mutual respect to allow the model of design and production to proceed.

As a final thought, a reason for this schism may lie in the use of the word "research" rather than referring to those in pre-production activities and "development." The term research has become associated with "ivory-tower academia" and being "out of touch with reality," both of which are totally misleading. Producers might not be as reluctant to work with analysts if they were retitled to bear a more direct relation to the program efforts.

General Omissions

In general, the sources on development in ITV appeared to be concerned with television as a means for mass distribution. This can be seen in the meaning of cost-effectiveness discussed previously, and in the concern of administrators to create a program which can be used in more than one instance. A second assumption is that some time period exists prior to the production of a program in which the program could be systematically planned and all related elements considered. The intent of this section is to show that both of these beliefs are not necessarily valid across all potential uses of ITV, and that the identification of developmental procedures based on other uses of television and limited or no planning time has not been undertaken.

Television as a technology has other unique properties besides the ability to reach a large number of people simultaneously in different locations. The capability of television to present events live, as they are occurring, to learners has been of seemingly little concern to ITV developers. The need, however, appears to exist. Prynne (1972) noted that television in medical education places a producer in the position of having to make many decisions about program content as the program is being shot. Kosoff and Mahrer (1973) noted the experiences of Florida public television in attempting to produce daily programs originating from the Florida State Legislature. The purpose of the program was to provide Floridians with more immediate information on actions taken by their representatives. But the time limitation for program preparation was short (less than a day)—barely time to make meaningful decisions based on learner and content characteristics.

The ways in which the problems of realizing an event while it is happening appear to be handled by commercial network television may provide some clues to developers and producers as to how ITV might approach the situation. If one were to view a "planned" spontaneous event via television, such as the Apollo-Soyuz docking, it is immediately evident that, first, as much pre-planning as possible went into the program: uses of mock-ups, to simulate occurrences which cameras may not be able to capture directly; the assigning of personnel who have become "content experts" to co-host the coverage and to describe the actions taken or to explain unanticipated changes; the use of a moderator or "TV figure" who has a background of experience in working with his audience. Basically, the set-up is one of a content expert and a learner expert working in conjunction to provide the viewer with as much of an actual account of the experience as possible in a presentation which attempts to be as meaningful to the viewer as possible.

In some cases the educator may not be aware of his reasons for wanting to show an event to his students as it occurs. Yet, it would be wasteful not to provide the experience when the producer suspects that there are values in the experience. Much immediate perception of content and on-the-spot decision-making is needed under such circumstances. No real solution is suggested here. The question posed to developers is whether they should forfeit a systematic approach to program development due to an insufficient time element for preparation. It is perhaps a challenge to developers to become intimately familiar with television's capabilities and constraints as well as with design and development considerations so that optimum program effectiveness can be obtained for all potentials of the TV medium for education.

In addition, the rise of new developments in television (e.g., two-way audio/video, dual audio, disc, etc.) provides ITV developers with more advantages and questions about the potential of televised instruction. A developer who ignores the impact of the technology is not using all possible resources in designing a quality instructional program.

Finally, the impact of television in combination with other strategies has not been of great concern. It is questionable how many programs have been abandoned as ineffective when they might have been effective if combined with some other strategies. Developers, especially in their formative efforts, need to be open to experimenting with the program at hand in combination with discussion groups, community resources, telephone feedback, etc., based on suspicions that certain combinations may increase efficiency and effectiveness.

References and Suggested Readings

Adams, P.D., *Evaluating Non-Commercial Television: A Case Study.* Austin, Texas: Center for Communication Research, University of Texas at Austin, 1971.

Advisory Council of National Organizations. *Public Broadcasting and Education: A Report to the Corporation for Public Broadcasting.* Washington, D.C.: March 1975.

Agency for Instructional Television. *Life-Coping Skills for Eleven-to-Fourteen-Year-Olds: Prospectus.* Bloomington, Indiana: AIT, 1974.

Agency for Instructional Television. *Dual Audio Television Instruction.* Bloomington, Indiana: AIT, February 1975.

Blakely, R.J. *Use of Instructional Television in Adult Education: A Review of Some Recent Developments.* Syracuse, New York: ERIC Clearinghouse on Adult Education, January 1974.

Bretz, R. *A Taxonomy of Communication Media.* Englewood Cliffs, New Jersey: Educational Technology Publications, 1971.

Bretz, R. *et al. Models of Television-Based Educational Programs: A Draft Report.* Santa Monica, California: Rand Corp., August 1971.

Briggs, L.J. *Handbook of Procedures for the Design of Instruction.* Pittsburgh, Pennsylvania: American Institutes for Research, 1970.

Brown, J. Instructional developer for AIT, Bloomington, Indiana, unpublished interview of September 4, 1975.

Brown, P.J. Odyssey in Black: A New Role for ETV. *Educational and Industrial Television,* November 1972, 19-21.

Brown, R.D. *et al. Evaluation of a Variety of Television Lesson Formats for Potential Adult Learners in an Open-University System.* Lincoln, Nebraska: University of Nebraska, 1973.

Bruner, J.S. *Toward a Theory of Instruction.* New York: Norton, 1968.

CTW Review 1973-1975. New York: Children's Television Workshop, 1975.

Carlson, R. *Possibilities and Limitations of Cable TV for Adult Education.* Speech presented at the Federal City College Conference on Cable TV, Washington, D.C., April 1974.

Carpenter, T.H. *The Utilization of Instructional Television in Music Education: Final Report.* Greenville, North Carolina: East Carolina State University, 1969.

Cavert, C.E. *Instructional Television Service in the United States: A Composite Profile.* Lincoln, Nebraska: Great Plains National Instructional Television Library, 1972.

Cavert, C.E. *An Approach to the Design of Mediated Instruction.* Washington, D.C.: AECT, 1974.

Coleman, E.B. *Management Plan for a National Effort in Reading.* Paper presented at the American Educational Research Association Annual Meeting, 1971.

Davies, I.K. *Competency-Based Learning.* London: McGraw-Hill, 1973.

Di Vesta, F.J. *Instructional Strategies: A Model and Its Applications, Annual Report, Pt. 1.* University Park: Pennsylvania State University, Department of Educational Psychology, July 1971.

Dorn, W.S. Technology in Education: A Case Study of the Open University. *International Review of Education,* 1974, *20*(1), 63-70.

Dudek, L.J. What Entertainment Television Has to Teach Instructional Television: A Communications Model for Improving In-School Television. *Educational Technology,* April 1972, *12*(4), 40-43.

Flaugher, R.L. *Report on Evaluation Activities of the Bread and Butterflies Project.* Princeton, New Jersey: Educational Testing Service, 1974.

Gagne, R.M. The Analysis of Instructional Objectives. *Instructional Design: Readings.* M.D. Merrill (Ed.) Englewood Cliffs, New Jersey: Prentice-Hall, 1971, 102-118.

Gillett, M. *Educational Technology.* Scarborough, Ontario: Prentice-Hall of Canada Ltd., 1973.

Gillom, B.C. and A. Zimmer. *ITV: Promise into Practice.* Columbus, Ohio: State Department of Education, 1972.

Grayson, L.P. Costs, Benefits, Effectiveness: Challenge to Educational Technology. *Science,* 1972, *175,* 2-3.

Hall, G.L. Letter From Wingspread. *Public Telecommunications Review, 3*(2), March-April 1975, 2-3.

Hawkridge, D. *Media Taxonomies and Media Selection.* Milton Keynes, England: Institute of Educational Technology, The Open University, 1973.

Herd, J.R. "Commercials" That Instruct and Entertain. *Educational and Industrial Television,* March 1973, 21-24.

Himmelweit, H.T. Education and Broadcasting: A Perspective. *Educational Broadcasting Review,* December 1971, 45-53.

Hood, P.D. and J.N. Johnson. *The Development and Evaluation of a Television Workshop in Human Relations.* Berkeley, California: Far West Laboratory, 1969.

Ives, J.M. Research in Educational Television. *Programmed Learning and Educational Technology,* July 1971, *8*(3) 161-172.

Joyce, B.R. *Television and Social Studies: Synergy and Symbiosis.* ERIC, 1971.

Kitzens, E. and H. Knox. *Britian's Open University: A Report to the Task Force on External Studies of the University of Pittsburgh.* Pittsburgh, Pennsylvania: University of Pittsburgh, 1972.

Kosoff, D. and N. Mahrer. Covering the State Legislature: How It Happened in Florida. *Public Telecommunications Review,* August 1973, *1*(1), 35-37.

Leonard, D.H. and J. Roberts. Asking the People About the People's Business: Public Television. *Educational and Industrial Television,* March 1974, 26-29.

Lesser, G.S. Assumptions Behind the Production and Writing Method in "Sesame Street." *Quality Instructional Television.* Wilbur Schramm (Ed.) Honolulu: University of Hawaii Press, 1972.

Lesser, G.S. *Children and Television: Lessons from "Sesame Street."* New York: Random House, 1974.

Loasa, L.M. *"Carrascolendas": A Formative Evaluation.* Los Angeles: University of California, 1974.

Low, D.S. *The Instructional Development Factory.* Provo, Utah: Brigham Young University, 1973.

Lumsdaine, A.A. "Content" and the Outcomes of Educational Programs. *Quality Instructional Television.* Wilbur Schramm (Ed.) Honolulu: University of Honolulu Press, 1972.

Lundgren, R. What Is a Good Instructional Program? *Quality Instructional Television.* Wilbur Schramm (Ed.) Honolulu: University of Hawaii Press, 1972, 6-22.

McElreath, M.P. Developing a Strategy for Adult Education Via Mass Media. *Adult Education*, 1974, *25*(1), 23-33.

Merrill, M.D. Components of a Cybernetic Instructional System. *Instructional Design: Readings*. M.D. Merrill (Ed.) Englewood Cliffs, New Jersey: Prentice-Hall, 1971, 48-54.

Mielke, K. *Decision-Oriented Research in School Television*. Bloomington, Indiana: AIT, September 1973.

Mielke, K.W. The Federal Role in Funding Children's Television Programming: Executive Summary. Institute for Communication Research, Indiana University, Bloomington, 1975a.

Mielke, K.W. Lecture on Evaluation for "Feeling Good," May 1975b.

Millard, S. Specialized Audiences: A Scaled-Down Dream? *Public Telecommunications Review*, October 1974, *2*(5), 48-54.

Molenda, M. *Instructional Television in Higher Education*. Bloomington, Indiana: Indiana University, 1974.

National Academy of Engineering, Advisory Committee on Issues in Educational Technology. *Issues and Public Policies in Educational Technology*. Lexington, Massachusetts: Lexington Books, 1974.

National Instructional Television Center. *Continuing Public Education Broadcasting*. Bloomington, Indiana: NIT, 1969.

Niemi, J.A. *Mass Media and Adult Education*. Englewood Cliffs, New Jersey: Educational Technology Publications, 1971.

Niemi, J.A. *Possibilities and Limitations of Cable TV for Adult Education*, speech presented at the Federal City College Conference on Cable TV, Washington, D.C., April 1974.

Palmer, E.L. Formative Research in Educational Television Production: The Experience of Children's Television Workshop. *Quality Instructional Television*. Wilbur Schramm (Ed.) Honolulu: University of Hawaii Press, 1972, 165-186.

Park, W.S., Jr. Three Grand Old Dames. *Educational Broadcasting Review*, April 1973, 102-104.

Perry, J. and J.D. LaBarr. Indiana University Instructional Television Service, unpublished interview of August 26, 1975.

Popham, W.J. *Systematic Instruction*. Englewood Cliffs, New Jersey: Prentice-Hall, 1970.

Procedures for Instructional Design: Proceedings of the 1972 Lincoln Leadership Conference on Instructional Design. *Audiovisual Instruction*, October 1972, 8-15.

Project Strive. New York: Corporation for Public Broadcasting, April 1972.

Prynne, T.A. *Handbook on Hospital Television*. Columbia, South Carolina: Educational Resources Foundation, 1972.

Rivlin, Alice M. *Systematic Thinking for Social Action*. Washington D.C.: Brookings, 1971.

Rogers, E.M. and F.F. Shoemaker. *Communication of Innovations: A Cross-Cultural Approach.* New York: Free Press, 1971.

Schramm, W. What the Research Says. *Quality Instructional Television.* Honolulu: University of Hawaii Press, 1972.

Seguin, E.L., C.A. Lindsay, *et al.* Program Audience Profiles. *Educational Broadcasting,* May/June 1974, 29-31.

Seibert, W.F. Broadcasting and Education: ERIC/EBR Annual Review Paper. *Educational Broadcasting Review,* June 1972, 139-150.

Shively, J.E. *Educational Television Personnel's Review of the Technical Quality, Content Criteria of AEL's "Around the Bend."* Charleston, West Virginia: Appalachia Educational Laboratory, 1973.

Stowe, R.A. and T.M. Schwen. Varieties of Analysis in Instructional Development. *AVCR,* Spring 1973, 5-10.

Thiagarajan, S., assistant director for instructional development, Center for Innovation in Teaching the Handicapped, Indiana University, Bloomington, Indiana, unpublished interview of August 27, 1975.

Tosti, D.T. and J.R. Ball. A Behavioral Approach to Instructional Design and Media Selection. *AVCR,* Spring 1969, *17*(1), 5-25.

Tyler, R. Persistent Questions on the Defining of Objectives. *Instructional Design: Readings.* M.D. Merrill (Ed.) Englewood Cliffs, New Jersey: Prentice-Hall, 1971, 89-96.

U.S. Senate Appropriations Committee. *Hearings on Funding for H.E.W. and Related Agencies, Pt. 7: Non-Departmental Witnesses,* July 10, 12, 16, 1974.

Van De Bogart, E. North of Namaskeag: A Viewer-Active Television Project. *Educational Broadcasting,* November-December 1972, *8*(7), 23-28.

Warren, K. Good Educational Programs Take Time, Money and Expertise. *Educational and Industrial Television,* March 1974, *6*(3), 17.

Webster, J., former researcher for "Feeling Good," unpublished interview of September 1, 1975.

Weiss, C.H. *Evaluation Research.* Englewood Cliffs, New Jersey: Prentice-Hall, 1972.

Welliver, P.W. A Systematic Approach to ITV Curriculum Development. *Educational Broadcasting,* May/June 1972, *5*(4), 11-13.

Wholey, J.S. *Federal Evaluation Policy.* Washington, D.C.: Urban Institute, 1975.

Williams, F. *et al. "Carrascolendas": National Evaluation of a Spanish/English Educational Television Series.* Austin, Texas: Center for Communication Research, University of Texas at Austin, 1973.

4.

A Cognitive Approach
to Media

Gavriel Salomon

What is it in the new media, indeed in instructional means and learning environments in general, that could possibly make a meaningful difference in learning?

Why, for instance, should instructional television (ITV) be any better than live teaching, multimedia presentations better than single-medium ones, or—for that matter—"open" classrooms better than "traditional" classrooms?

[There are at least three factors which could make a difference in learning: The *technology* involved, the *content* transmitted and the *symbolic codes* into which the messages are coded.]

Technology and Transmission

The technology of transmission has been studied and researched in hundreds (if not thousands) of investigations. However, not much has been found that merits to be mentioned. It just happens to be the case that technology of transmission qua technology simply does not make any meaningful difference in learning (Mielke, 1968).

There are, of course, numerous *obvious* findings. Some technologies reach large populations and are therefore considered more effective, but this advantage they have is neither unique (the

Gavriel Salomon is Associate Professor, The Hebrew University of Jerusalem, Israel.

printed book was the first medium to reach wide audiences), nor is it particularly inspiring. A medium whose sole advantage is the improved distribution service it provides is, of course, a "better" medium, but one need not be a university graduate to discover *this*. Some media permit the student to control his own learning pace, whereas others provide the instructor with more control over his students' learning activities. But, again, this makes just a *trivial* difference in learning. For one thing, ITV is expected to entail more than just a better distribution service of instructional packages.

Look at the question of technology (content and symbolic code of messages presently disregarded) from still another point of view. Children who face difficulties with reading do not read any better or worse if the material is *printed* rather than *projected*. Changing the technology through which the material is transmitted to them makes no difference. Similarly, a televised instructional session is no more effective than a live one simply by virtue of its being televised. And why should it be?[Neither research nor theory (nor even good old-fashioned common sense) warrant the hypothesis that technology *per se* makes a difference.] The same, it appears, applies to specific technological components such as color ITV vs. black and white, distance from screen, and the like (Chu and Schramm, 1967).

Content

[Different media have different information potentials by virtue of both their technologies and the symbolic systems available to them. Thus, whereas one medium will be better suited to "handle" a particular range of contents, another will be more capable of carrying another range of contents.]Indeed, the content of a message (and issues related to it, such as novelty, familiarity, complexity and difficulty) do make a difference in learning. But the difference in learning which different contents (or different levels of difficulty of content) make are either self-evident or unrelated to media. They are self-evident whenever we find that, say, ITV can show a "real" event (e.g., how a community gets organized) whereas another medium cannot. If having a vivid image of such an event is considered desirable, ITV will quite obviously be "better." But, then, isn't it self-evident? Differences in learning caused by different contents are often also unrelated to media. Some contents may be found to have more "appeal," or to be more thought provoking, than others. Presenting such contents on ITV may be less costly, or more convenient, but this says nothing about any *inherent* attribute of ITV. The fact that particular contents excite or provoke has nothing to do with the medium.

The Symbolic Code
of the Message

Finally, let us consider the symbolic codes used in messages. There are no "raw" messages, since an idea once made into a communicable message is by definition a *coded* idea. Whether put into words or graphemes, into moving images or body movements, into a musical score or into numerals, it is *always* coded. Codes differ as to how basic and "pure" they are. Some, such as language, pictorials, numerals, etc., are more basic and only peripherally related to specific technologies. Others are more complex codes, composites of other codes or highly sophisticated derivations of basic codes. They are more strongly related to specific technological innovations which make them possible. Television is a prime example of a medium whose symbolic code is based on other codes, and on new derivations made possible by recent technological advances in the field of TV. Such a medium has a vast system of symbolic codes available to it. Some of the system's codes are shared also by other media (e.g., film, photography), but there are some which are the unique creations of this medium.

[*It is the code into which an idea is coded that makes the*   ⬅ *largest and most important difference in learning.*] We learn, as Stoddard once remarked, not by doing but by thinking about

what we are doing. Indeed, there is now ample evidence to show
that what generates learning and governs it are the *mental
processes* activated by the instructional stimulus. Hardly any
learning takes place without the mediation of mental processes.
But these, in turn, are strongly affected by the ways messages are
coded (Olson, 1974). In other words,[*the nature of the symbolic
code of a message affects the mental skills with which the
information is processed.*]Thus, a verbal description of an object
and a picture of it do not differ only in appearance, they also call
upon different mental skills which are then used to process the
conveyed information.

In a recent study (Salomon and Cohen, 1976) five versions of
the same TV program were produced. The versions did not differ
as to the content (it was one and the same) but rather in terms of
the major TV code, or format, which was utilized in each version.
Thus, whereas one version was based on numerous zoom-ins and
zoom-outs, another version displayed fragmented spaces, another
version used logical gaps and still another was based on many
close-ups. Clearly, these are but simple TV codes, or formats. Yet,
analyses of the mental skills called for by the film very clearly
showed that each version played to different kinds of skills. No
wonder, therefore, that the knowledge acquired in each case was
different in amount and in content. Thus, for instance, children
viewing the version which emphasized close-ups acquired more
knowledge pertaining to the relations between parts and wholes.
On the other hand, children viewing the version which entailed
logical gaps excelled in their comprehension of the plot's logical
structure and continuity.

It becomes rather clear that one cannot deal any more with a
single "medium" as a unitary entity. Each medium has a wide
range of symbolic codes at its disposal. *Each combination of such
[codes may have different effects on mental skills, or processes.
These cognitive effects, in turn, determine the way the material is
processed and learned.]*

Individual Differences

Once specific media attributes are considered in light of what cognitive effects they have, it becomes a necessity to consider individual differences among learners. Learners differ as to their mastery of those mental skills called upon by different media-generated codes or formats. In the study quoted above it was found that those who learned most from each version were the children who had the best mastery of the *relevant* mental skills. If a program such as "Sesame Street" calls upon, say, one's skill of interrelating discontinuous program-segments, then those children who have not yet mastered this skill face difficulties in attaining interrelatedness of segments.

Effects and Effectiveness

We should now distinguish between the cognitive *effects* of a particular, medium-generated combination of codes (i.e., the mental skills they call upon), and their *instructional effectiveness*. Effect and effectiveness are not to be interchanged. A highly variable, quick changing, multi-screen display like "Where's Boston," arouses specific mental skills in the information processor. These are the show's *effects*. But are they also instructionally effective? This depends on the nature of the learning task. The effects produced by that show could be effective if emotional appeal is the instructional objective; the effect is ineffective if one wants the audience to acquire a well structured body of informational facts about Boston.

Assertions

It becomes possible to assert the following:

1. Media differ in terms of their technologies of transmission, contents and symbolic codes.

2. Technologies of transmission *per se* make hardly any difference in learning; contents make a difference but are not part and parcel of the media; *it is the symbolic code into which a message is dressed that affects learning.*

3. Codes (i.e., message formats) affect learning inasmuch as they call upon different modes of information processing, that is, mental skills, which in turn govern and produce learning.

4. Learners differ as to their mastery of the relevant mental skills, and hence, cognitive effects of media attributes interact with individual differences.

5. The effectiveness of a presentation depends on the match between the mental skills activated by the presentation's code, or format, and the requirements of the learning task.

An Hypothesis

The cognitive approach thus far outlined leads us to the following general hypothesis:

Media of instruction, or any combination thereof, is effective in teaching to the extent that the symbolic codes used in its messages affect cognitive skills which are relevant to the learner's mental capability and to the requirements of the learning task.

"Sesame Street," when shown to then TV-naive Israeli children, had rather strong cognitive effects. It facilitated the cultivation of particular mental skills, without which processing of the program's novel formats would be difficult. The program thus played to the relevant cognitive capabilities of Israeli children. However, these cognitive effects were only partly relevant to what the learning of the program's *content* seemed to require. Hence, no wonder that it was not very instructionally effective (Salomon, 1976).

It is now quite easy to see why so many of the ITV vs. live-teaching studies failed to detect any systematic differences in favor of one or another method. If such comparisons are methodically well done, all variables aside from the mode of presenting the instructor are held constant. But then, is there any unique difference of code (format) between the live and the televised session? Indeed, there is none and *only the technology* used is allowed to vary. The mental processes called upon by both modes of instruction are similar, if not identical, and hence produce the same learning results.

If, indeed, ITV is allowed to show its very best, and to utilize *its* unique formats, one could expect *other* mental processes to be affected. And if those are more relevant to the cognitive (or emotional) requirements of the learning task, and more relevant to what the learners can or cannot mentally perform, ITV would be more effective than another medium, given *that* task and *those* learners.

ITV has some unique potentialities which, when properly utilized, can facilitate learning. These potentialities reach beyond the technological nature of the medium or even beyond the contents it is so well suited to transmit. They are inherent in TV's large arsenal of codes. In what follows *one* such potentiality, recently investigated, will be described.

One of ITV's Potentialities

[One of TV's major advantages is its capability of overtly and explicitly showing a *process*, a *transformation*. Many other media present transformations (language included), *but TV alone can visually show a transformation which is analogous, or even similar, to what ought to take place in our minds*. In other words, TV can overtly simulate a process which otherwise would have to be executed covertly in thought.] Take for instance the act of zooming-in. This is a transformation by means of which a particular detail is being singled out from a wider and richer array. The zoom provides the link between the long shot view and the close up. In the absence of the zoom, the viewer is required to provide the same link covertly on his own. The zoom, when used, simulates overtly the same process. Gradual changes of angles, rotations in space, rapid shifts, split screens, and the like, have the potential of accomplishing the same function: They *overtly supplant* a mental skill, transformation or, if you wish, process, for the learner.

There are two major possible consequences to the function of visual supplantation, namely, the facilitation of learning and the cultivation of relevant mental skills. Let us examine the two. If learning is indeed governed by the arousal and activation of particular mental skills, and if not all learners are equally masterful of the skills, then a presentation which overtly supplants the necessary skill should compensate for the learner's deficiency.

[Take learning of geometry of objects as an example. To master geometry, the learner needs to be able to visualize certain movements of objects in space, as well as imagine three dimensionality in its absence. A child who has not yet mastered these mental skills cannot learn well the content of geometry. But then imagine an ITV program which overtly supplants these transformations; objects rotate in space in this program, and otherwise hidden sides become visible. It would not be surprising to find that such a show enhances the acquisition of knowledge in geometry by learners who could not acquire it without the overt supplantation.]

[The important point to notice is that a *particular* element of TV's store of codes is being utilized here, allowing it to accomplish a specific cognitive function which for some children is most effective in learning.]Recent findings of ours strongly support the example provided above (Salomon and Cohen, 1976).]

[But the enhancement of the acquisition of knowledge is not the only function that supplantation accomplishes. Overtly supplanting a specific transformation leads also to an improved covert mastery of that skill. Thus, e.g., children who watch many such spatial rotations on the screen become better able to visualize these rotations mentally, even applying them to new instances (Rovett, 1974). Interestingly enough, it is a rather consistent case that such cultivations of mental skills take place mainly in children who start out with poor mastery of the supplanted skill (Salomon, 1972; Salomon, 1974).]

In sum, then, media do something to the minds of learners: Media's symbolic codes call upon mental skills or (as in the case of TV) they may supplant them. These are the *effects* of the media. By calling upon or supplanting mental skills, the media may facilitate the acquisition of knowledge or even cultivate skill mastery. To the extent that such functions are accomplished, media may be said to be effective. Notice, however, that the examination of media's instructional potentialities, as discussed here, necessarily calls for a cognitive outlook. How else can we understand and make intelligent use of the potentialities of ITV?

References

Chu, G.C. and W. Schramm. *Learning from Television: What the Research Says.* Stanford, California: Stanford University Institute for Communication Research, 1967.

Mielke, K.W. Questioning the ETV Question. *Educational Broadcasting Review*, 1968, *2*, 6.

Olson, D.R. Introduction. In D.R. Olson (Ed.) *Media and Symbols: The Forms of Expression, Communication and Education. The Seventy-third Yearbook of the National Society for the Study of Education.* Chicago: University of Chicago Press, 1974.

Rovett, J. Can Spatial Skills Be Acquired Via Film? An Analysis of the Cognitive Consequences of Visual Media. Unpublished Doctoral Dissertation, University of Toronto, 1974.

Salomon, G. Can We Affect Cognitive Skills Through Visual Meida? *AV Communication Review*, 1972, *20*(4), 401-422.

Salomon, G. Internalization of Filmic Schematic Operations in Interaction with Learners' Aptitudes. *Journal of Educational Psychology*, 1974, *66*(4), 499-511.

Salomon, G. *Sesame Street in Israel: Its Educational and Psychological Effects on Children.* Jerusalem: The Hebrew University, 1976.

Salomon, G. and A. Cohen. The Effects of TV Formats on Mental Skills. Paper presented at the Conference on Visual Literacy, International Visual Literacy Association, Nashville, Tennessee, March, 1976.

5.
Instructional Television: Do We Have the Courage to Succeed?

Paul Bosner

In addressing the question of instructional television's implementation by the educational systems and processes of the United States, I think it is necessary to probe areas heretofore given insufficient attention; the massiveness of the system; the decentralization of the system; and the fragmented, overlapping funding structure of the system which results in obscured centers of power resting somewhere between state and local control, with subtle direction by the federal government.

Why these areas have not been given greater importance and significance as they relate to the implementation of ITV troubles me. It is almost as if they have been avoided. Even the recent Carnegie Commission report, *The Fourth Revolution*, makes only limited reference to these problems. Yet, it is precisely in this area that the ultimate success or failure of ITV to become institutionalized will be determined. The fact is that the rooms full of data which continue to accumulate, concerned with the effectiveness of ITV versus traditional teaching methods, will not determine acceptance of ITV as a vital part of our educational process. This data was and will continue to be valuable and important, and there are ample researchers and scholars who will continue to seek the new and refine what exists, but the practical decisions of ITV's acceptance will not be based upon their findings.

Paul Bosner is Managing Director, Television and Educational Classics Ltd., London, England.

What is ITV? It is the application of the methods and technology of television applied to purposeful instruction; the results of this process are carefully designed, validated and empirically tested materials. The essential purpose of ITV is the dissemination of teaching to large audiences. This task requires the combined skills of a large team of educationalists and television practitioners over a period of years at a possible cost of several million dollars for one series. ITV is not a savior nor a cure-all, but it can be very effective and exciting when its application is correct.

Presently schools plan and budget on an annual basis. Though there are minimum required areas to be covered in a discipline, there is no uniformity of curriculum from school to school, let alone from district to district or from state to state. Obviously, ITV will require a totally different attitude about education as well as a maturity on the part of those who control it; for, in the implementation and institutionalizing of ITV, gross inadequacies in existing and past educational methods and practices will be revealed.

It is more than a coincidence that the State University of Nebraska, the Coast Community College Districts of California and the British Open University have all had to go outside the traditional college structure to develop an original institution capable of coping with the many innovative demands that arise when media in general and television in particular become an integral part of the pedagogic experience of an institution.

Television Systems and Schools:
Different in the U.S.A.

Quite often when successful models of ITV implementation are referred to, there is a decided absence of U.S. models. Reference is usually made to activity in England, Sweden, Japan, Israel, France and to a number of projects in developing and emerging countries. It is significant that there is one factor common to all these examples; their educational systems are nationalized, controlled by a Ministry of Education, with the power center of pedagogic and budgetary control centralized at the apex of an educational bureaucracy. Such systems have other problems common to a civil servant bureaucracy, but the implementing of innovative practices deemed necessary to the furthering of their educational objectives is not one of them.

In the U.S. there are nearly 17,000 public school systems containing some 92,000 public schools and 2,500 universities, colleges, and community and junior colleges. More than 90 percent of the funds required to operate this variety of schools comes from local and state taxes, and about 60 percent of this amount comes out of the community in which the school is located. Though this educational system may leave a lot to be desired, it is massive beyond anything or societies could imagine or afford.

That education is a very big business can be little questioned. The 1974-75 national expenditure for education was more than $50 billion. It is also estimated that if education continues to operate as a cottage industry, the cost of this inefficiency, at the current rate of growth plus the inflation factor, will by the year 2025 equal the current gross national product, $1 trillion 300 billion, an almost incomprehensible figure.

Implementation

Thus far I have addressed myself very little to the question of implementation of instructional television but rather to some of the problems of education, because what we are confronted with are educational systems problems, not television problems. In addressing and then attempting to solve these problems television and technology will find their proper role and the question of implementation will resolve itself. It is impossible to look upon ITV as a thing apart from education. At some point education as a business will be obliged to examine itself; to ask the classic, often avoided questions (education is not unique in this avoidance): "What business are we in?" "Are we performing in the best possible manner to achieve our goals?" "How must our enterprise change if our goals have changed?" But in reality who is going to

ask these necessary questions? The massiveness of our decentralized system makes "education" an abstraction. There is no one
system but many thousands of systems throughout the U.S.A.,
mostly controlled by politically vested interests rather than by
those with a singular commitment to what is educationally
expedient. Idealistic, utopian perhaps, but ultimately such a
commitment will be required to properly deal with the problems
of a seventeenth century methodology functioning in a twentieth
century society.

Because old myths will be debunked, classic institutions will
need to be restructured, and new skills and fresh thinking
demanded of our educators, the personal and professional insecurities of many will continue to surface in protest and resistance. So
be it. The conflict of the old and the new in all things is painful
and unavoidable, though intelligence and a clear commitment to
one's purpose can minimize the disturbing effects of transition.

Toward Economic Feasibility

How do we get the educational system of the United States
to a scale small enough to manage yet large enough to make the use
of instructional technology that is now economically feasible?
Initially a task force should be created of state and federal
representatives for the purposes of determining regional educational districts consisting of contiguous states. A regional district
would be controlled by a pedagogic committee comprised of
commissioners of education of the states within that district. This
committee would have the power and the authority to determine
those disciplines and curricula which would have a large audience
and wide application best served by ITV or some other form of
appropriate technology. It is at this stage of development that
roles must be clearly defined for regional, state and local
involvement as it applies to curriculum planning and uniformity of
programs. There then would follow for modeling purposes the
development of one regional district, encompassing all the tasks
and bureaucracy involved in creating a technologically oriented

educational system to serve the needs of that district. Each regional district would have its own instructional technology center committed to producing the media materials required for the participants in that district.

It might be thought that existing public television stations might very well be the producing agencies for the media required for the regional districts. My opinion is that this is a poor idea, for a number of reasons. This kind of undertaking requires a singular commitment, specially trained personnel and a facility of substantial size. For example, to produce 175 to 200 program units a year, either videotape, film or a mixture of both, plus the writing and production of appropriate support materials, will require a staff of at least 200 people (subject consultants, producers, directors, production secretaries, production assistants, script writers, music director, film crew personnel, editors, engineers, TV cameramen, audio men, stage crew, set designers, carpenters, model makers, scenic artists, graphic artists, animation artist, makeup artists, costumers, researchers and evaluators, plus an adequate administrative staff to manage all of the above) and a facility containing at least two studios which will be in use every day. I don't know of any public television station in the country that could properly commit itself to such a venture; in addition, public television has its own unique problems of survival with which it is trying to contend.

Such an undertaking will require much federal funding, arm twisting and persuasion. This grand consortium effort suggests change on many levels, all of which is practical and achieveable. Emotions will soar; the flag will be waved; traditions of the past will be restated. A great deal of the reaction will be sincere but perhaps much of it will be a mask obscuring vested interests, insecurities and a reluctance to relinquish power. Direction and leadership must come from the federal government. The magnitude of the tasks to be dealt with requires a vision far greater than that of most locally elected citizenry.

I cannot see a course much different from that described if a serious use of television technology is considered as a means of bringing the educational system into the twentieth century at a cost that the economy can tolerate. Is it possible that the country that placed a man on the moon and returned him to earth will have difficulty discovering the educational wheel?

6.

A Working Model for Instructional Television

Jack McBride

Instructional television has traveled several academic miles since its introduction to the American educational scene, since the Creighton University prefreeze experiments, since the first Western Reserve telecourse, the initial Carpenter-Greenhill Penn State CCTV research, the Fund for the Advancement of Education schools improvement projects, since Hagerstown, Frank Baxter's Shakespeare in not-too-vivid black and white kinescope, since the Harvey White EBF physics series.

Or has it? An analytical look at instructional television in the United States would indicate that it has not fulfilled its sometimes too boisterously pronounced promise and potential. True, all but the most biased critics would concede American education is the better for ITV. But, for all the investments of time, effort, resources and dollars at the various educational levels, the qualified success stories are too few in number.

There are important exceptions and bell-weather developments—significant ones—such as: the American Samoan opportunity to restructure the curriculum to the television medium; the initial Chicago TV College outreach successes; the sharing of improved instructional television products such as *Parlons Francais* and *Places in the News* through such distribution agencies as the

Jack McBride is Executive Vice President, University of Mid-America, Lincoln, Nebraska.

Great Plains National Instructional Television Library; MPATI's crossing state boundaries; and the new consortial funding productions of the Agency for Instructional Television/National Instructional Television. Campus CCTV systems, such as at Ohio State and Michigan State University, have become increasingly integral to the resident instructional mission. State networking, as in South Carolina, Kentucky, Ohio and Nebraska, in conjunction with departments of public instruction, is affording both an improved ITV program and more direct integration with the elementary/ secondary construct. Regional public television networks have begun promising ITV programming cooperatives. Significant public television offerings like *Forsyte Saga, Civilisation* and *America* have spurred ITV improvement. Consortial development by the Texas Educational Microwave Project, the Indiana Higher Education Telecommunications System and the Nebraska Educational Television Council for Higher Education point the way to increased sharing among institutions.

Faculty receptivity toward television and the other educational technologies is improving. The various national disciplinary journals and conference agendas now regularly include media in their discussion topics. Accrediting agencies now approve mediated instruction, and educational administrations now regularly include media line items in their budgets. New and improved production facilities are taking their rightful place in schools, on campuses and at Public TV stations. As a result, U.S. educational institutions carry a major investment in equipment, facilities and ITV services. Videotape recording, ITFS and cassette improvements have abetted ITV usefulness; cable and satellite developments promise even more.

But for all the investments of time, effort and money, for all the equipments available, for all the research and evaluation results (so many of which report "no statistically significant difference"), for all the experience at all the educational levels, ITV is unfortunately still too peripheral to instruction, is still too sparingly employed, particularly at the higher levels. Faculty apathy is still too evident. The quality of the instructional television program is still hampered by a lack of sufficient and intelligent academic and professional media input, as well as by unrealistic budgets. The complexities of employing ITV still obtain. And the perennial problem of training both users and practitioners is still with us. Despite the many problems which have these past two decades plagued ITV and delayed fuller achievement of a potential still real and ever-present, this writer prefers to remain optimistic. Two far-reaching, substantive and impressive success stories, the Children's Television Workshop and the British Open University, are serving as harbingers to those laboring in the electronic and educational vineyards and as models for future development.

The Children's Television Workshop's evolvement, its *modus operandi* and its successes have been widely chronicled. Not so specifically reported is an important dividend. Through "Sesame Street" and "The Electric Company," CTW has given ITV three important legacies. First, CTW showed academicians, administrators and funding agencies that a major capital investment in design and production is necessary to achieve quality courseware. Secondly, CTW was the first to depart from the televised instruction format—where television was an add-on to content treatment—to adopt an instructional television process designed specifically to the medium. And, thirdly, CTW showed that content, research and professional production can be effectively combined. For this, American ITV will forever be in its debt. The "Sesame" and "Electric Company" landmarks have already generated a variety of improved production techniques at the local ITV level, and will for years to come be responsible for quantum improvement in the ITV product.

The initial and continuing successes of the British Open University are likewise an ITV milestone, and serve as a prime stimulant to renewed interest of higher education in the media and to open learning planning and development in every section of the United States. The OU course development team, which brings academicians, instructional designers and media professionals together to develop mediated instruction addressing specific educational objectives, will be emulated for years to come. Similarly will be their approach to non-traditional instruction, their deliberate combination of correspondence study, television and radio, and their systematic employment of the mails, computers and regional learning centers to compensate for the loss of the teacher at the head of a classroom.

The SUN and UMA Model

It is within this context that the State University of Nebraska (SUN) and the even newer University of Mid-America (UMA) have come upon the educational scene as another possible developmental model of some potential. In order to consider the potentiality, a look at the history, purpose and organization of the two agencies is appropriate.

The State University of Nebraska was formed in 1971, in response to a University of Nebraska study of the recommendations of the Carnegie Commission on Higher Education and of the Newman Task Force. During the first two years, this new project was supported by grants from the U.S. Office of Education, and particularly from the National Center for Educational Technology. In this planning period, strategies for the design and delivery of mediated adult education were studied at length, and experimental lesson modules were developed and tested. Three market and clientele surveys of the potential audience for open learning were commissioned. The resultant data uniformly showed that a significant percentage of the adult population was sufficiently interested in postsecondary education to enroll and pay tuition. SUN subsequently received major grants from the National Institute of Education to complete an elaborate series of specific work assignments directed toward completion of planning for a multiple-year regional open learning experiment.

During 1974, a carefully developed economic model was commissioned to assess the economic implications of various operational procedures. This model, together with an equally detailed five-year cash flow model developed by SUN, provides the fiscal basis for the proposed plan of experimental operations.

In order to broaden its economic base of operations, increase its potential target audience and assure that the open learning program reaches the widest possible learner market, SUN investigated formation of a regional consortium. The plan developed was found to be both advantageous and feasible, and the University of Mid-America was in July of 1974 incorporated on a non-profit basis specifically to undertake the regional production and dissemination of open learning courseware, and to coordinate development of delivery systems in at least the states of Missouri, Iowa, Kansas and Nebraska. Iowa State University, the University of Kansas, Kansas State University, the University of Missouri and the University of Nebraska are the charter participants in UMA. Bylaws were specifically written to encourage future additional participation or organizational change as needed. UMA is thus developed as the operational base from which a model regional open learning system can be administered and tested.

UMA is in fact neither a university in the usual sense (it has no resident faculty or campus) nor an external degree program (it offers no degrees or credits). It is a means of providing learners, on their own terms, with a rich variety of postsecondary learning opportunities which can be used to meet differing individual interests or the educational needs of specific groups of adult learners.

Development of open learning delivery systems is the responsibility of each participating state, with the advice and assistance of UMA. The SUN delivery system in Nebraska, already developed to the point of initial operation, serves as the testbed for system design and as an operational model which might be studied by the other cooperating states. During 1975, the other states comprising UMA systematically developed statewide delivery system plans, to enable phased activation in 1976. They will make use of existing delivery resources and operating postsecondary programs to meet individual needs.

The SUN delivery system in Nebraska has been designed to take advantage of the nine-station statewide public television network. Newspaper space is provided for lessons as a public service by the state's largest daily and other cooperating newspapers. Printed materials, audiotape cassettes and instructional kits forwarded via the mails, a 24-hour inward telephone toll-free WATS line and a network of learning centers are among the other Nebraska open learning elements. It is anticipated that the other UMA states will capitalize upon such local features as cable television, public radio, computers and university extension services to insure that the open learning program in each state has maximum flexibility, efficiency and accessibility.

A major element of the delivery plan in Nebraska is a statewide network of regional learning centers which provide a direct link between the adult learner and the delivery system. Four such centers are currently in operation on an experimental basis, each initially staffed with a specially trained coordinator/counselor and an assistant. These new facilities are available to learners for tutorial and remedial assistance and counseling, and provide additional access to course materials (such as videotape cassettes of television components). The centers free the adult from constraints of broadcast schedule and academic calendar. The centers also serve an important clearinghouse function as a source of information about other educational opportunities, both in the community at large (libraries, local postsecondary institutions, museums and art galleries), and on a larger scale (educational programs and services throughout the region and nation). Moreover, these centers serve the important function of providing feedback from learners for use in both curriculum planning and course development.

UMA's curriculum planning is complicated by the diverse, non-traditional and quasi-anonymous nature of its target audience. No single set of assumptions holds true for all members of this adult population, which ranges from the high school senior wanting a head start on college to the senior citizen interested in a particular content but not for credit. Some individuals seek college credit, others do not; some seek professional advancement, others basic education; some are motivated by practical interests, others by recreational. Thus a number of orientations toward curricula are necessary, if UMA is to serve the sub-groups in its target population.

SUN's pilot deliveries of its first courses have afforded UMA's Office of Research and Evaluation a unique opportunity to study in operation the various open learning delivery system elements, and to learn much more than is currently known about the nontraditional learners to be served.

Planning a curriculum requires more than the selection of a list of courses; it requires understanding of learner and societal needs and desires, and of the intended relationship among courses chosen for development and delivery, and the use of these courses by learners. A curriculum, then, presumes some kind of ordered (but not necessarily rigid or uniform) educational experiences which, in the aggregate, represent a logical cluster of goals, content and pedagogy. UMA proposes to provide at least four general categories of educational experiences to help serve the diverse subpopulations: college credit courses for those seeking credentials; inservice vocational or professional training courses; skill courses for personal improvement; and non-credit personal enrichment courses. Each of these categories embraces a variety of possibilities, and in many instances these categories overlap (for example, a practical nurse wanting paraprofessional or inservice training might also desire college credit).

The UMA Academic Council, composed of academic and academic-administrative staff members from the five UMA universities and chaired by the UMA Vice President for Academic Affairs, prepared during 1974 a detailed Open Learning Goals Statement and a tentative list of courses for development over a five-year period. The UMA Open Learning Goals call for the provision of educational experiences which allow the student flexibility in constructing his own learning sequence and permit the reduction of constraints on how people can learn.

Special attention has been given to the development of courses, and over a four-year period SUN/UMA has designed and tested a new concept and process. UMA is committed to using a variety of media to meet the non-traditional learner on his terms, to attract him, to retain him. Television, audiotape cassettes, film, newspapers and the print medium have been researched and evaluated by SUN in experimental lesson components, and these media have been systematically employed in the first courses completed. Future plans call for consideration of such other media as broadcast radio and computer-assisted instruction.

Experienced professional production personnel working creatively at the Nebraska Educational Telecommunications Center aim to bring to UMA course production a new level of ITV quality. The Accounting course, for example, has a three-time Emmy award winner as producer-in-residence, an Emmy holder as television writer, and another as audio writer-director. New York and Hollywood talents serve as actors and presentors. The same Lincoln production facility houses the largest and most experienced media distribution service of its kind, the Great Plains National Instructional Television Library, which will manage the national distribution of UMA materials as they become available. The media components of future UMA courses will also be produced at other UMA production facilities.

UMA has a specially designed course development process, which includes different approaches to both design and team composition.

The complex and systematic instructional design procedure can be summarized in five steps: design, production, field testing, re-design and re-production. A resident content specialist, aided by a senior content advisory panel, is joined by an instructional designer, a producer, writers, a researcher-evaluator and television, audio, film, graphic, print and design specialists for the life of the course. This enables content, design, production and evaluation to work together creatively as an integrated team.

The aim is not to produce rigidly structured traditional courses, but materials which allow the learner to mold individual opportunities according to unique individual needs. In order to provide maximum flexibility, UMA will stress development of interdisciplinary courses, modular offerings which allow the student to follow various tracks through them, and other structural variations designed to meet individual needs.

Five different approaches to the design of non-traditional educational experiences have been identified: development of courses which include a high-cost television component; development of courses which include a low-cost television component; development of mediated courses without television; acquisition of existing courses for use with minimal adaptation; acquisition of existing courses requiring major adaptation. Time lines and budgets have been developed for each approach. Courses will be developed according to the five approaches, with a preponderance of the acquired variety either adapted or used intact. The acquisition of extant materials allows UMA to develop a large number of courses at the lowest possible cost; but standards of quality dictate that the majority of acquired courses probably will undergo some adaptation before they are employed.

UMA was designed to reach a large group of adults and to achieve economies of development and delivery. A central development agency can use pooled resources, thus enabling the creation of courses and materials of a quality and quantity which could not be produced by a single state agency. Furthermore, the courses developed can be used by adults in a number of states, thus providing a learner population much larger than that available in any single state.

Though UMA is a reality, a number of issues related to consortial development remain to be resolved: whether a regional open learning consortium should itself be a credit or degree granting institution; to what extent the consortium should be expanded; by what process states associated with UMA can be assisted to develop open learning delivery systems; how UMA courseware can be most effectively exported within UMA states and outside the UMA region; and how the UMA governance structure and procedures can be refined with sufficient flexibility to deal with questions of curricular choice and delivery based upon data from learners.

One major task facing UMA is enacting its plan for consortial funding, whereby money from NIE, from other public agencies, from private foundations and business, and from course leaseage and student tuition is combined to finance the operation of this regional open learning system. The multiple-year plan as developed sees the basic UMA support from NIE lessening as the developmental period progresses, and supplanted by increasing contributions from the UMA states and income from courses leased nationally. SUN will operate through tuition income and state appropriations.

This presents but a brief glimpse into an elaborate and complex plan which is challenging, exciting, timely and potential-laden, yet at the same time is highly experimental and subject to all of the problems of a path-finding venture. What is described represents several years of extensive planning and research. There is reason for optimism, and firm conviction to employ educational media in a non-traditional approach to serve this special and important adult audience.

If this new approach to course development—using multiple media, systematically working from pre-stated educational objectives, employing special course teams of content, research and media specialists, validating the educational product, and having sufficient budgets to permit an academically sound and professionally mediated product—can be proven effective at the postsecondary level, the approach can be employed at any educational level and with any instructional objective. The University of Mid-America and the State University of Nebraska could thereby become the newest working model to effectuate substantive and rewarding improvement in American ITV.

7.

College Credit Courses by Open-Circuit Television

Linda S. Agler and
Theodore W. Pohrte

The Dallas County Community College District, a large multi-campus institution with four colleges located in downtown Dallas and surrounding suburbs, offers college credit courses by open-circuit public television to over 10,000 students annually. Of the eight courses offered during the 1975-76 academic year, four were developed by the District: "It's Everybody's Business" (Introduction to Business), "Writing for a Reason" (English Composition), "Communicating Through Literature" (Composition and Literature) and American Government. All are basic courses central to the college-level, transfer programs typically offered by community junior colleges. Each carries three semester hours of transferable credit.

In addition, courses in earth science, humanities and American history are presently under development.

Telecourse Components

The instructional television (ITV) courses constitute a learning system having several components which combine to form a multifaceted learning experience. Following registration, attendance is required at an on-campus orientation session designed to

Linda S. Agler is a Research Specialist in the Office of Special Services, and Theodore W. Pohrte is the District Instructional Development Specialist, Dallas County Community College District, Dallas, Texas.

introduce students to the course and their on-campus TV instructor. The ITV programs usually consist of 30 half-hour lessons delivered at the rate of two a week. Each telelesson is aired at least three times during the week, on different days and at different times of the day, to better accommodate the student's schedule, since most of the TV students work part-time or full-time. A study guide provides lesson overviews and objectives, vocabulary, outlines of the TV programs, study exercises, support materials, optional activities and self-tests. One to three optional on-campus discussion meetings are scheduled to give students an opportunity to meet with their on-campus TV instructors, obtain answers to their questions, and interact with other students. A "hotline" telephone information service is maintained in the ITV Center through which students may obtain course information and be put in contact with their instructors. Textbooks or readers are purchased by students from the college bookstore. Newsletters which keep students up-to-date on the course are sent periodically. Three to four examinations are scheduled on each campus during the term. These examinations are taken under proctored conditions in central test centers.

The ITV Center is responsible for the development and production of course materials. The Center has found the application of a systematic approach to instructional design, when employed by trained instructional development specialists, results in the production of high-quality courses with very acceptable learner success. The ITV Center approaches instructional design in a carefully planned sequence to ensure the development of instructionally effective course materials. A variety of experienced specialists assists in the development and review of materials during the process. A schematic representation of the development process is shown in Figure 1, and a chart of the ITV Center organizational structure is presented in Figure 2.

Telecourse Selection

The deans of instruction of the four colleges of the District

Figure 1

ITV Course Development Chart

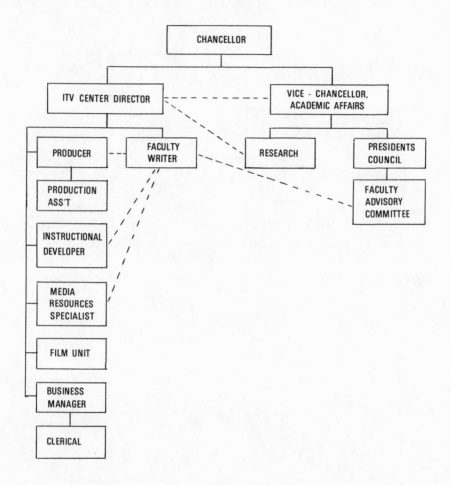

Figure 2

ITV Center Organizational Chart

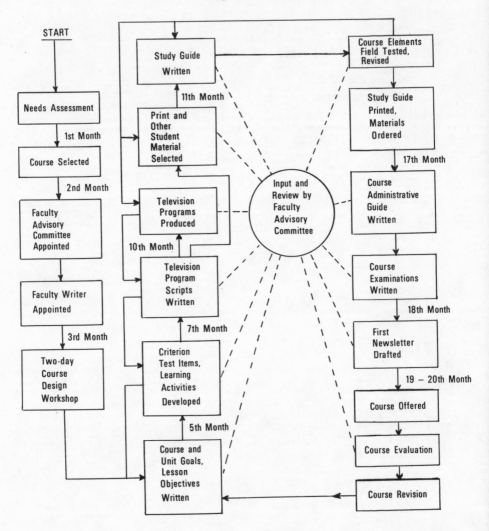

and the director of the Instructional Television Center explore the feasibility and desirability of offering a particular course by television and make a recommendation to the four college presidents. The recommendation is based on the following criteria:

1. Course enrollment projection—is it likely to be sufficiently high to justify the development and operation costs?

2. Suitability of the subject matter to an open-circuit, ITV delivery system—is it likely to be at least as effective as traditional instructional modes?

3. Subject matter of the course is worthy of three to four semester hours of college transfer credit—does it fit the established pattern of a basic college-level course, and would the credit be transferable to senior institutions?

If the course is approved by the Presidents Council, each president appoints a faculty member from the subject area to an advisory committee for the telecourse. The process of instructional design begins with a needs analysis conducted by the advisory committee based on data available from the district research office and other sources. The main purpose of this analysis is to determine the characteristics of the potential student population and the appropriate learning goals of this population. Once these goals are identified, the ITV Center investigates the possibilities for the leasing of appropriate programs, study guides and other materials that are in successful use elsewhere. If such materials are found, the process described below is altered to focus on the development of any needed support materials for the course and course management procedures.

Telecourse Design

If the decision is made to develop the course from the beginning, the first task of the ITV Center is to convene the faculty advisory committee for a two-day course design session. Prior to the design session, one of the faculty members will have been appointed by the Vice-Chancellor of Academic Affairs as the committee chairperson and faculty writer for the course. During the first day of the session, the committee's task is to define the principal goals of the course based upon post-course competencies which are determined by the needs analysis. Decisions are made regarding the course philosophy, and the major content areas for the course are delineated based upon committee consensus. On the second day, the principal goals are subdivided into units and unit goals are written. Feasible learning materials and activities are explored. Consideration is also given to the manner in which the various course components may be utilized most effectively; for example, the role and function of the ITV programs, the study guide, textbooks and readers.

The next stage in the ITV course development calls for the establishment of a development team. The development team consists of the faculty writer, one of the Center's professional television producers, an experienced television production assistant and a television script writer with considerable experience in writing materials for commercial or educational TV programs. At the same time, a support team is assigned to the project which includes a resources specialist, an instructional design specialist, experienced television filmmakers and editors, and clerical staff.

The development and support teams are responsible for refining the course goals and other ideas which were developed during the design session. They are also charged with developing a timetable for course completion. The faculty writer takes the lead in refining learning objectives, developing criterion-referenced test items and structuring learning activities on a lesson by lesson basis. As this material is developed, it is circulated to the advisory committee members for their comments. The faculty writer assembles the advisory committee periodically for additional suggestions and assistance in developing the materials. It has been found that this emphasis on the development of test items and learning activities at the beginning stages of the course development results in a closer match of instruction to the lesson objectives and keeps the writer's attention focused upon the desired post-course competencies.

Telecourse Development:
TV Programs

When consensus on the lesson objectives, activities and test items has been reached, the faculty writer works with the television program development team to produce the 30 scripts. The faculty writer is primarily responsible for developing the content. The producer and script writer modify and interpret the material to adapt it to instructional television. The faculty writer, however, retains final authority over the content of the TV programs. Under the direction of the producer, the production assistant arranges filming of segments in the field and taping in the studio.

Typically, TV programs utilize a variety of audio and visual elements intended to motivate, to illustrate, to highlight, to summarize and to reinforce. Use is made of film, on-camera talks, on-location interviews, panel discussions, dramatizations, demonstrations, simulations and animations. In most cases narrators are professional actors, although faculty may appear on camera on occasion. It should be noted also that the television component of the course system carries only 30 to 50 percent of the content burden; the balance is carried by the print materials the student has in hand.

Telecourse Development:
Study Guide

After the film and studio production is well underway, attention is focused on the study guide and other print material. Since lesson objectives have already been specified and topic outlines for the ITV programs have been completed, much of the material for the study guide already exists. The faculty writer now focuses on developing lesson pretests and posttests for inclusion in the study guide. These self-tests, based on the lesson objectives, serve to help students assess their entry and terminal mastery of the lesson objectives. The faculty writer also develops additional background information for the study guide where such information is required. This usually includes additional vocabulary lists, in-depth explanations of difficult or particularly significant material, essential ideas not adequately presented in other elements of the course, and supplementary activities designed to encourage active rather than passive participation on the part of the learner. As the faculty writer completes lessons they are circulated to the members of the advisory committee for comments and revisions.

Telecourse Management Procedures

When the study guide and ITV programs are completed, the faculty writer meets with the advisory committee to solicit suggestions for the writing of a course administration guide. The guide will later serve as a policy manual for course administrators and instructors to ensure consistency in the handling of the course from campus to campus and to facilitate student progress through the course. It is planned that at this point in the process, field testing of lessons will be undertaken for telecourses now under development.

Finally, the faculty writer begins drafting the first of several newsletters which will be sent to students during the term. The main purposes of the newsletter are to advise students on how to study for the course and complete any assignments, to alert them to any changes in the broadcast schedule of ITV programs or in the administration of examinations, and to keep them up-to-date on course happenings.

After the development of all course components has been completed, the advisory committee members conventionally become the on-campus TV instructors. They are responsible for orienting students to the ITV course, answering student questions, keeping student records, leading discussion meetings, and grading examinations and assignments. During implementation of the course, the ITV Center provides support services: airs the ITV programs, disseminates newsletters, operates the hotline, prepares and distributes tests, and performs other activities helpful in the administration of the course.

Telecourse Evaluation

By the time the course is first offered, the District Research Office finishes plans for assessing course effectiveness to determine what revisions will be needed. Information on course weaknesses and strengths generally comes from four major sources: (1) records are kept of student calls to the hotline telephone service to determine which kinds of questions are occurring most frequently; (2) records are kept of student calls to their instructors to determine which content areas are causing students the greatest difficulty; (3) surveys are administered to students to determine their views of course strengths and weaknesses; and (4) evaluative models are developed and instituted to assess the relative achievement of ITV and on-campus students, to assess entry and terminal mastery of the course objectives, to follow up successful course completers to determine their progress in subsequent courses, and to contact withdrawing students to determine their reasons for dropping the course. The ITV Center is responsible for obtaining and analyzing the data from the first two sources. An independent research analyst working in the District Research Office is responsible for the third and fourth categories.

Based on the formative evaluation data, emergency revisions are made. Based upon the summative evaluations, major course revisions are usually made after the first full year of operation. Thereafter, minor revisions are made as needed for the life of the course, which is usually three to five years, depending on the subject matter.

Development System Advantages

Among the major advantages of the course development system employed by the Dallas County Community College District are: (1) While several experts are employed in the course development process, each of whom maintains direct responsibility in a specified area, development occurs as a joint effort in which the experts are provided ample opportunity to meet and interact with one another. (2) The group process encourages a commitment of the advisory committee members to the final product; this is particularly important since the ultimate success of the course depends heavily on the effectiveness and dedication of the individual campus instructors. (3) While most of the course development activities proceed sequentially, some activities can be carried out in parallel; this ensures that the over-all process proceeds according to schedule even if problems occur at some point in the development process. (4) Finally, the provisions for editing and revising the course ensure that flexibility is maintained and that an improved instructional system is available for each successive offering.

8.

ITV/ETV Evaluation:
What We Should Expect

Frederick Williams and
Monty C. Stanford

It is not difficult to make excuses for ITV/ETV evaluation. For one thing, it got off to a bad start. Most studies involving the use of television for educational purposes up until the mid-1960s were simple comparisons of some existing live instructional activity with its direct videotaped or filmed reproduction. Few attempts were made during this period to evaluate the unique qualities that the television medium might hold for instruction (Chu and Schramm, nd). Also, it was difficult enough for educational planners and production people to work together, even without the problem of giving evaluators a major role on a project team.

Despite this late start, it appears as if evaluation of educational television has enjoyed a relatively positive growth since the mid-1960s. Again, circumstances probably played a major role. The heightening of social awareness (and funding) associated with the War on Poverty and other programs of this period increasingly attracted researchers as well as research organizations into the educational area. Controversy over the supposed effects of educational projects and the general call for accountability stimulated the growth of evaluation efforts. Finally, the success of the "Sesame Street" project, which had a visible evaluation component, heightened awareness of the potential for evaluation of ITV/ETV (Lesser, 1974).

Frederick Williams is Dean and **Monty C. Stanford** is Assistant Professor, the Annenberg School of Communications, University of Southern California, Los Angeles.

Currently, most major projects involving the use of television in education have research components, including several commercial projects. Also (and the focus of this article) there is the accumulation of a number of generalizations about this type of evaluation—specifically, kinds of evaluations which are available to us, and what we should expect from them.

Types of Evaluation

Although consideration of types of evaluation can lead to a number of academic definitions (or arguments), we prefer to take a relatively practical and simple view of the matter. Most evaluation in this area means that, at best, an attempt is made to derive some generalizations about a program or its effect, based as objectively as possible upon observations. Generally the term "evaluation" implies some attention to a good-bad or even a success-failure type of generalization. But, much of the research of the last decade has involved (1) assessments of variation within the television medium, rather than simply comparing it with "live" presentations; (2) the simultaneous assessment of multiple aspects of a program and its effects; and (3) questions of degree more than ones of the "success-failure" or "good-bad" type. Thus, for example, rather than asking whether a television tape of a biology lecture will be as effective as, or better than, a live lecture, the more recent approach would be to make comparative assessments of variations in the televised version. Assessments would focus on a variety of aspects, including variations in the content, the production treatment, the viewing audiences and perhaps even the conditions under which the program is viewed. Assessments of degree may be in terms of performance tests, information gain measures, scales measuring attitude toward content and production, and even gauges of the attentiveness of students to the materials.

The approaches just discussed are also seen in differentiations between what is now for the most part called *formative* as against *summative* evaluation (Ball and Bogatz, 1970; Bogatz and Ball,

1971). Formative evaluation refers to assessments undertaken during the development of a program, where prototype versions are pretested on samples of the intended audience. As the name implies, the results of such research are entered directly into the formation process of the series. By contrast, a summative evaluation refers to those types of larger scale field projects where the effects of an already completed series are gauged during its application to an audience. These are after-the-fact types of assessments to see whether a program does indeed realize its intended impact. These two types of research might best be differentiated in terms of the practical questions which they answer. Formative research is tied to the question, "What responses to a particular segment will provide implications for further production treatments?" Summative research answers the question, "Does the series have the intended over-all effects on its intended audience?"

What Is Evaluated?

This point has already been made, but for most of the 1950s and early 1960s, the focus upon what was to be evaluated was conceptualized most often as a general $S \rightarrow R$ relationship, or:

Medium $\rightarrow$ Learning

In these studies, the question was whether a particular program or segment affected learning in an anticipated way. The effect was usually gauged by some type of objective (multiple choice) test, which might also readily be applied in an experimental comparison of a televised lecture against a live one. This type of approach is representative of so-called "bullet theory" approaches to media efforts, now often fashionably attributed to almost all types of media research in the 1950s. The trend beginning in the 1960s has been to focus evaluation upon a more multiple-variable conceptualization of what is to be evaluated (Williams and Van Wart, 1974). That is, the process of mediated instruction is viewed as a complex multifaceted process and not simply one of "push-pull," "hypodermic needle," cause-effect.

This shift toward a multiple-variable view incorporates not only multiple aspects of the instructional medium itself, but also characteristics of the respondent, the context in which the instruction takes place and a hierarchy of response measures. Certainly, not all studies include such a highly elaborate conceptualization, but the trend is toward taking into account all possible variables which may simultaneously and interactively be relevant to effects.

Thus, in contrast to the S → R approach, the view is more of the type shown in Figure 1.

The "Sesame Street" research team, for example, in their formative research activities, popularized a strategy for gauging the attention qualities of segments. This strategy involves showing children slides intended to compete for the children's attention while they were exposed to the program or segment being studied (Palmer, 1969). The practical rationale was that a television segment would have to gain a child's attention before it would have the chance to do anything else, and the attention eliciting qualities of segments should receive high priority in formative research. In a number of studies there has been a similar detailed interest in such other facets of response as the degree to which a student basically comprehends what is presented to him as preliminary to remembering the materials, using them in some type of task performance or having attitudes affected in some way.

In part the research interest in variables such as attention and comprehension has come about because researchers (and probably even project officers representing funding sources) have become far more practical and modest in terms of specification of changes. It is ironic how many studies have specified major changes in IQ as a result of media exposure in an instructional program. If a child, for example, watched a half-an-hour program three days a week this would constitute somewhat less than two percent of his waking experience per week. It is difficult to see how the program could produce changes in a characteristic as broadly defined as IQ.

Figure 1

Media Variables		Context Features		Student Characteristics		Effects
	+		+		=	
Content Variations		Viewing Environment		Age, Sex		Attention
Channel Variations		Viewing Frequency		Baseline Knowledge		Comprehension
Production Variations		Associated Activities		Cultural Background		Attitude
Etc.		Etc.		Etc.		Etc.

The current multi-variable approach to instructional media evaluation attempts to account for the combined influence of media, context and student characteristics in producing multiple effects.

Researchers have been more inclined to scale down their expectations, anticipating, for example, that mediated materials will achieve attention and comprehension at the least. Then, given these, one could expect recall or the acquisition of new skills, attitudes, and the like.

Research in the past decade has also revealed a number of highly relevant contextual variables affecting response to televised instruction (Stanford, 1973). These have included such practical considerations as the nature of the viewing environment (size of television set, number of viewers, acoustic qualities of the room), the degree to which "warm-up" activities are presented prior to viewing instructional media, the degree to which instructional media are directly articulated with curriculum in classroom activities, or more generally the degree to which instructional media are complemented with live instruction by the teacher or conversation with a parent or sibling in the home.

The point here is not to attempt to enumerate all of the possible variables that might be studied, but to emphasize that the trend in evaluation has been toward viewing communication involving instructional media as a complex interaction of factors rather than a simple stimulus-response relationship. Simultaneous with the more thorough and detailed delineation of what is to be measured has come an increased emphasis on the concept of behavioral or instructional objectives. Simply stated, such objectives are nothing more than a descriptive statement of some observed effect of the program—for example, "After viewing the program, the student will be able to draw and correctly label the face of a clock," or "After viewing this series, the student will be able to diagnose and repair the 10 common malfunctions of home TV receivers delineated below (etc.)." If the criteria for stating behavioral objectives are followed on a project, then such objectives form a common language among a program proposer, the producer, educational planners, the script writers, the director, the teachers who may use the program in classes and the evaluators who will assess the program's accountability. That is to say, given the clear goals of a project as stated in instructional objectives, these form a set of operational definitions for what the educational designer specifies to be accomplished, what the media producer must try to accomplish, and what the evaluator can assess in order to gauge the degree to which the goals of a project were accomplished. Considerable literature is already available on instructional objectives (Bloom *et al.*, 1956; Mager, 1962), and this is readily adaptable to media production, as can be seen in a number of projects.

Behavioral objectives lend themselves quite usefully to formative as well as summative evaluation, as mentioned earlier. In the earlier stages of the development of particular segments of the program, formative evaluation can be gauged against instructional objectives, with revisions made until the objectives are realized in test behavior. Similarly, the anticipated over-all effects of a series can be gauged in a kind of perfection fashion simply by sampling from among the instructional objectives in formulating test or observational criteria.

The use of instructional objectives among program proposers and educational planners has been particularly noteworthy in regard to the concept of *baseline data*. Here it is assumed that if certain behavioral objectives are proposed for a specified population, it should be possible to test beforehand the degree to which that population already exhibits the desired behavior. Or, in another perspective, when a prospective group is studied in terms of their educational needs, instructional objectives can be built upon what would presumably be the next step from baseline. Thus, instructional objectives are basic links in the entire process cycle for the identification of the need for particular educational objectives, the specifications of what a particular instructional program should accomplish, specifications that form a common language among all persons who are producing and developing the program and finally as bases for the final, or summative, accountability of the program.

Toward Modeling
Evaluation Results

Given the specification of measurable objectives and the multiple-variable perspective of contemporary evaluations, evaluation data usually lends itself to analysis by multivariate statistical techniques. Consider, for example, the following (hypothetical) equation expressed in a generalized form:

Viewing frequency + child's age + teacher experience + class size = Learning Gains

Equations such as the foregoing allow us to generalize the multiple effects of clusters of variables pertaining to program, student or context characteristics relative to performance of specified behavioral objectives. Given equations for objectives in a particular project, it is possible to generalize the degree to which objectives were obtained, and even to test such levels of attainment against the statistical or chance hypothesis. Beyond this it is possible to see the degree to which learning is attributable to the interaction of any cluster of factors in the equation. And a further use of the equation is that it can be used for predictive purposes. That is, if other groups of children may be identified with the children represented in the test sample, it will be possible to predict effects on these other groups, and further how those effects may vary according to other variables included in the equation. Such equations might even transcend this use when we think of them as accumulating from study to study. Thus, it may be possible eventually to make generalizations about the effects of production characteristics on learning across a great variety of studies or the interaction between production characteristics and content, type of children, and the like. In fact, if measures became relatively similarly defined across studies, it would be possible to pull data from studies and eventually to generate master equations that would test such aforementioned relationships including studies themselves as variations.

In all, the activities in the area of instructional television have begun to assume a relatively predictable process character outlined in Figure 2. The three stages in this process where the evaluator's work is critical are in baseline evaluation, formative evaluation and summative evaluation.

Systems Planning,
Yet Creativity Too

Lest we overlook a hazard found in many educational accountability strategies, there is considerable danger in planning by objectives leading to a "mechanistic" quality in ETV or ITV media. It is not difficult to find media projects which are "over-managed." They may be within budget, on schedule and models of PERT chart excellence, but they are devoid of any creative or artistic merit, and usually deserving of the public label "educational stuff." As evaluators, we would argue that the most successful ETV or ITV projects have been managed so as to stimulate creativity, not to stifle it.

A Final, Practical Note

We hope we have made the point that ETV/ITV evaluation has come of age. We can think of no valid reason why any project

Figure 2

*ITV/ETV Program Development
and Evaluation Process*

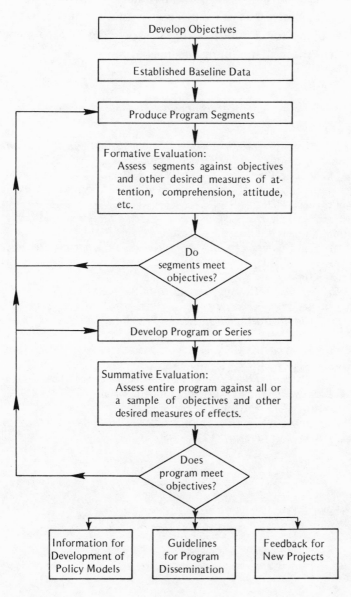

in this area should be allowed to proceed without having an integral functioning evaluation component. Certainly compromises might have to be made in the extent of evaluation and in the balance between the needs for formative and summative assessments. But to organize ITV/ETV projects without evaluation is to admit to no plans for accountability. It would be akin to going into business without maintaining financial accounts.

References

Ball, S. and G.A. Bogatz. *The First Year of Sesame Street: An Evaluation.* Princeton: Educational Testing Service, 1970.

Bloom, B.S., M.D. Engelhart, E.J. Furst, W.H. Hill and D.R. Krathwohl. *Taxonomy of Educational Objectives. Handbook I: Cognitive Domain.* New York: David McKay, 1956.

Bogatz, G.A. and S. Ball. *The Second Year of Sesame Street: A Continuing Evaluation.* Princeton: Educational Testing Service, 1971.

Chu, G.C. and W. Schramm. *Learning from Television: What the Research Says (Rev. ed.)* Washington, D.C.: National Association of Educational Broadcasters, nd.

Lesser, G.S. *Children and Television: Lessons from Sesame Street.* New York: Random House, 1974.

Mager, R.F. *Preparing Instructional Objectives.* Palo Alto, California: Fearon, 1962.

Palmer, E.L. Research at the Children's Television Workshop. *Educational Broadcasting Review,* 1969, *3*(5), 43-48.

Stanford, M.C. *On Predicting the Effects of a Bilingual Children's Educational Television Program.* Unpublished doctoral dissertation, University of Texas at Austin, 1973. ERIC ED 082 498.

Williams, F. and G. Van Wart. *Carrascolendas: Bilingual Education Through Television.* New York: Praeger, 1974.

9.

Instructional Television:
The Medium Whose Future Has Passed

Dave Berkman

It's not that instructional television—indeed, I would submit *all* of instructional technology!—is dead, for one cannot attribute death to that which has never shown life.

This is a verity—at least as it applies to the role of technology in formal, in-school instruction—which those of us willing to face overwhelming reality must admit as true.

These, let me stress, are not the recreant rantings of an apostate technologist. I am surely as true a believer in the intrinsic goodness and worth of the centrality which instructional technology would seem predestined to occupy in our schools as is any amongst that pantheon of media saints and ETV ecclesiastics who have sat and worshipped at the feet of Marshall of Tornoto or his apostle John, ex-of-Fordham. I look upon a Skinner box as I would gaze upon the Holy Grail and would regard a Pressey device as the most precious of relics. I revere the revelations in this journal as constituting a Gospel as sacred to me as is the writ of Mark, Luke *et al.*, to the Christians among my brethren. And I pray with an anguished fervor that the infidels among us, those pedagogues who worship only Gutenberg the Father while denying Marconi and (most appropriately) Zworykin, will recognize the errors of their narrow, non-Nicean ways. To switch these

Dave Berkman is Adjunct Professor of Communications at American University, Washington, D.C.

strained metaphors, momentarily, from the theologic to the literary, I find it Kafkaesque that some tens of millions of children emerge daily from a media-saturated environment to enter schools where they continue to be taught by the same insipid, tedious and all but totally non-electronic, labor-intensive methods which have debilitated youthful minds ever since collective wisdom first mandated that shutting young people up in a box, to be talked at, tested and turned off, constitutes the essence of good education.

Having thus made this profession of pure faith, I trust my Brothers in Technology will hear me out: for what I wish to give testimony to is not that the Coming of Technology, and specifically ITV, is not devoutly to be wished—but, rather, that at least as far as our schools are concerned, it just ain't never gonna happen.

If I were to seize upon one piece of evidence which would sum up the truth of what I am arguing, it would be to cite that Edsel of ed tech Edsels, the Instructional Television Fixed Service—or, as it is familiarly known to that handful of initiates who are on intimate terms with it, ITFS.

Common sense should tell us that if ITV were, in fact, of even the slightest significance in education today, ITFS would be at least as hot a medium ("hot" in the colloquial, not the McLuhan sense of the term) as, say, the teaching machine. If there were even the most minimal demand by our schools for instructional TV, the present ITV broadcast delivery system, which offers only one channel of service to meet the needs of one subject at one grade level at one time, would have had to find itself augmented by a rush to the multichannel, over-the-air system of ITV delivery which is ITFS*, and which the FCC established in

*For those who are not familiar with it, ITFS refers to an instruction-only TV service transmitting over a special set of television frequencies located above the UHF channels, in the 2500 megaHertz (or 2½ gigaHertz) band. Because these channels are located that high up in the spectrum, there is enough capacity to allow the licensing of up to four channels to a single school system or other instruction-offering licensee.

the mid-1960s to provide school systems with the means to transmit more than a single, over-the-air channel of ITV into their classroom. Yet, today, a decade after the ITFS service was inaugurated, fewer than 75 multiple-channel ITFS systems are being operated by the almost 17,000 school systems in the United States.

Bear in mind that the medium of which we are talking here is 30-year-old television—not, as so many ed tech people still so absurdly insist, one of those "tomorrow technologies" just lying in wait for the schools to discover it.

But why this rejection of television—a rejection analogous to science's or industry's rejection of the computer?

Actually, the situation is such that we can't even find something as encouraging as "rejection" to cite. To speak of "rejection" implies that the schools, at one time or another, were concerned enough about ITV to have thought about the matter and that they then made a conscious decision to turn it down. In fact, the situation was (and is) so bad that it was never even a case of rejection or acceptance. Rather, ITV, like so much of instructional technology, is so *outside the ken* of those teachers and administrators who populate the educational mainstream, that it's never even been considered!

The even more disheartening aspect of the situation is that however poor are the possibilities that ITV might be used in a significant manner, those chances are less today, and will be even less tomorrow, than was the case 10 years back.

It is a perception (prejudice?) of mine that many of us who consider ourselves to be in the vanguard of ed tech—and thus by definition as media proponents also hip!—tend to be awfully square and naive. We are victims, in fact, of that most classic of McLuhanist errors: rearview mirror vision.

Most technologists and other ITV proponents seem to think that all the medium needs to achieve its rightful place in the halls of learning is that we show its value—perhaps as a function of its cost- and/or learning-effectiveness—and pronto, those who make the decisions will lay ITV on the schools. Herein, however, lies that "rearview" error, for many such folks still entertain the quaintly anachronistic notion about the hierarchical nature of American education which assumes a-board-telling-a-superintendent-who-tells-a-principal-who-tells-a-teacher-what-to-do. (I know we're big on the rhetoric of participatory decision-making; but what we profess, and what we actually believe, may be two entirely different things.) What such archaic thinking ignores is that American education is becoming more and more teacher-dominated. And as education becomes more and more teacher-dominated, chances for ITV become slimmer and slimmer.

The reason for this increasing teacher-dominance is, of course, collective bargaining. And, as we approach the point where collective bargaining between teacher organizations and school systems is becoming the norm rather than the exception, the marching orders are coming from the bottom up.

It is teachers today who call the shots in schools because it is the collective bargaining contract which sets the rules. And rule No. 1 now for any principal who once sat atop his school and its pedagogical serfs like a feudal lord above his feifdom is, don't let a dossier of formal grievance procedures accumulate against you at school headquarters. Pity, therefore, any principal or other administrator who, for any reasons, enlightened or otherwise, attempts to lay anything on any teacher about what is to take place in his/her classroom!

It is this cataclysmic (but surprisingly little attended to) change in education, reversing the direction of authority 180 degrees, which lies at the nub of the problem: the very advantages ITV offers and which make the most positive arguments for its use are also the very factors which work most against its adoption. This is because these are also the advantages which conflict with the most vested interests—economic, but perhaps even more important, those that are ego-derived—which most teachers hold most dear.

If ITV ever did have a chance to take off, it was in the late

1950s through the mid 1960s. This was the era of the teacher and physical plant shortages, and of the mythic Crisis in Education. (Of course the real educational crises—which still exist—long antedated Sputnik, and had little, if anything, to do with the percentage of persons who would exit from our schools capable of taking their place next to Werner Von Braun.)

It was also the era when the Ford Foundation put some $25,000,000 into proving the worth of instructional television through the National Program for the Use of Television in the Public Schools. (Though, today, scant more than a decade later, I defy anybody to show me where this multi-megabuck-backed experiment—by far, still the largest ever in American education—rates even a footnote in the education texts.) If, given these conditions, all arguing for its acceptance, and with this massive Ford Foundation thrust behind it, ITV couldn't make it back then, why do we think that the time when TV will play even a minor role in formal learning is only a short time away?

Let's explore some of the reasons why the ITV thrust of the "education crisis era" failed, and see what these causes have to tell us about the situation now.

To a rather startling degree, and despite the history of failure not only of ITV, but of such ed tech "shticks" as PI and teaching machines, and the promotion of "The Systems Approach," many of the errors which the Ford folks and their ITV allies made then, continue to be made today.

Perhaps the most fundamental of these concerned a really incredible misreading of who teachers are, why they teach and, therefore, where they perceive their interests to reside—a misreading whose continuance dooms the proponents of in-school uses of TV and other technologies to their permanent status as a most minor sect within the theology of American pedagogy.

What those, whom one must assume were the most sophisticated minds money can buy, came up with as an approach to counter opposition to ITV, was a dual, but interrelated, campaign which, first, avoided anything which teachers might perceive as indicating ITV was out to displace them; and, second, centered on the hyping of a concept which can best be termed, "The Joys of Team Teaching."

The first error almost immediately sealed the fate of ITV, because it made unmentionable the key value of instructional television: that even at its worst it could teach at least as well as the classroom teacher*; at its best, far better. (If it couldn't, then why bother?)

But it's the "Joys of Team Teaching" thrust and its total disregard for the real world that I want to examine in some detail. (In many respects it's close to and only a bit less naive than much of The Systems Approach hype which one still hears ed technologists talking about to themselves.)

What it came down to is that ITV is a partnership composed of two equals: the studio teacher and his/her classroom counterpart, neither of whose roles was subservient to the other. Now one has got to assume that the Ford people and their ITV allies who propounded this scam had spent few of their days in a classroom

---

*At this time the writer was studying for his doctorate under Prof. Charles Siepmann, who was to Ford in its ITV days what Fred Friendly has been in the Public TV era. (Siepmann, it should be stressed, was among that handful who were aware of and concerned over the gaffes which others in and out of Ford were committing in their attempts to spread the ITV Gospel.) Prof. Siepmann had just completed a tour of all the centers involved in the production of TV materials for the National Program, and was quite disturbed in that of the sample programs he had seen, from each of the over 200 series in production, he found exactly one which he judged to be of acceptable quality. He was sure that when the experimental/control group comparative study results came in, they would show that ITV had bombed. But once they started arriving, they almost all showed, much to Siepmann's surprise, that the poor quality televised instruction proved equal—and where there was a difference it was usually ITV that was superior—to the traditional, face-to-face, direct method of instruction to which it was being compared. Needless to state, this seemingly inexplicable result bothered Siepmann for some time—until it suddenly dawned on him one day what the explanation was: no matter how bad the televised instruction, it was no worse than what normally passes for instruction in the classrooms of America!

teaching. Because, while *they* might call it team teaching, the classroom teacher knew what it really was, it was a kick in the rear! "I mean like it's got to be obvious to any of my kids watching me shut up while the TV teacher's talking, that if I was as good as him (her), then *I'd* be up there, and he (she)'d be sitting down here!"

Let me anticipate a point which I'm sure many of my readers are mentally making to themselves: that while this might have been true of the "Big Talking Face" ITV of the 1950s and early 1960s, today's teachers cannot possibly be demeaned by comparison to the sophisticated, high production value ITV of the mid 1970s. To which I'd respond first, that with few notable exceptions, ITV *hasn't* changed that much in 15 years; and second, that even if it had (or were to), it would still be naive to dismiss what I (at least) am coming more and more to see as the all-important "ego factors" which doom to failure any potential for significant use of ITV and any other of the non-frivolous educational media technologies.

If I am, say, an elementary school teacher, and you take away from me my role as The Provider of basal instruction in reading or arithmetic, then what you take away is the essence of my professional being—and no professional should have a greater interest than in protecting that which he or she regards as his or her most essential professional functions. This is the healthy side of what I would term the "ego factors." The other side is one which I am sure many of us suspect exists, but one whose existence we seldom give overt acknowledgment to, if for no other reason than that it isn't nice! Yet, the fact is that for many (most?) teachers, classroom teaching provides a less healthy, but extremely powerful, ego-enhancement insofar as the traditional face-to-face, direct method of instruction allows one to command the attention of 30 people (albeit 30 little people) for five hours per day. Few are the other occasions in one's lifespace when one can exercise such power. And few are those teachers who are going to give up any of that power to a talking picture box!

Until we recognize and begin to come to grips with the vested ego-interests inherent in traditional methods of teaching, we cannot realistically deal with the problems which surround the introduction of media into formal education. Otherwise, we will continue only to engage in the meaningless exercise of offering to the deaf ears of teachers what is only to us the terribly impressive statistical and experimental evidence proving how certain components of the instructional process—usually those which teachers find most ego-satisfying—best lend themselves to media-mediated presentation. Further, if I'm right in what I suggest about teacher-dominance, then it is of little practical import how successful we are in convincing such others as administrators, school boards or the community-at-large. (Besides, most of these others no doubt already find themselves more than comfortable with the traditional instructional methods which they themselves experienced as former teachers and/or as students. For here, too, we ignore that for all the concern which the Kohls, Kozols, Silbermans, or we as technologists, express about what's wrong with education, most people in or out of the schools find them pretty good. In fact, if the polls are correct, to the degree that there *is* dissatisfaction, this seems to be a dissatisfaction over the degree to which schooling has *departed* from the rigidities of the past!)

At this point, cognizance must be taken of the argument for the use of educational media in general, and ITV in particular, which rests on the assumption that the most effective use of such media is within an instructional strategy which, while taking away the teacher's basal expository role by assigning that to the media, frees him/her to assume the role of diagnostician of, and prescriber for, individual student strengths and weaknesses within the varying disciplines. In other words (and contrary to what I suggested earlier), convince a teacher that it's not exposition to the total class which is the essence of his/her professional being, but rather the highly skilled one-to-one and one-to-small-group relationship of teacher to pupil(s) which freedom from basal exposition allows, and you make a convert to instructional TV!*

Yet, before we could promote this seemingly practical and reform-laden approach, we would first have to ignore the previously cited ego-satisfactions inherent in basal exposition; and, second, accept the extremely tenuous notion that even if teachers want to be freed of their basal responsibilities so that they can devote themselves to individualized, diagnostically oriented work, that most are equipped to do so. Yet, how many teachers actually want to (or can?) relate to children on a one-to-one basis? How many are capable of making the finely tuned, highly specific and discrete diagnoses of extremely particularized learning skills or subject matter debilities which such a "freeing-up" presupposes they are equipped to make?

My bet is that the number is far smaller than we'd want to admit. In fact, I would strongly suspect that for many, if not most, teachers the greatest sense of security lies in the guaranteed safety which the inevitable bell-shaped curve of the total class-room situation provides; and that, for many, the greatest fear would be the risk of having any of their questionable or lacking skills exposed naked to the world—a risk one would take every time he or she had to relate to and work with a student in a small group or on a one-to-one basis.

All of the above, insofar as it speaks only to non-economic matters, doesn't even begin to deal with the fears, legitimate or otherwise, which teachers now operating in a buyer's market feel about educational technology as a threat to their job-security. Forget the sincerity of our denials that we are after teachers' jobs—although it seems to me that when we talk about cost-effec-

*This, essentially, is the approach known as the Stoddard Plan, and it is the approach which the Ford Foundation initially intended would underlay the adoption of ITV by the schools. Ford subsequently decided, however, that for practical PR reasons it could not push the mandatory use of ITV which the Stoddard Plan necessitated, and switched its promotion to one emphasizing the supplementary—and therefore optional—role of instructional TV.

tiveness we are talking about *someone's* job, and most certainly not our own—because if teachers (and their union officers) perceive ed tech as job threatening, then it is those perceptions, and not our protestations, that are all that matter.

This reference to "cost-effectiveness" brings to mind further examples of naivety (though, in these instances, frequently compounded, I would suspect, by compartmentalized thinking), engaged in by those among us who propound the cause and the case of ITV and related technologies.

For example, the effective use of instructional TV—as with any medium—demands (as does all good classroom procedure) adequate and often intensive preparation. This, I would think, at the very least should mean that before a teacher uses an ITV series in his/her classroom, he/she should preview its component programs. Now remember, we're speaking here of a medium, a chief argument for the use of which is its cost-effectiveness. But when is a large city, unionized teacher* to be expected to undertake that viewing, when the contract he/she works under carefully limits the after-school time which can be demanded of a teacher to one 40-minute faculty meeting per month, at 39 minutes and 50 seconds of which the union shop chairman gets up like the senior press association correspondent at a Presidential news conference, thanks the principal right in the middle of a sentence, and with the whole rest of the teaching staff following right behind, marches out! Given collective bargaining created conditions such as this, just when do we expect teachers to preview media materials? If after-school time is out, this means they would have to use time they now devote to teaching—which would mean making effective use of ITV *more* costly, *not* more cost-effective!

---

*I think I should hasten to make the point here that I am not anti-union. I have belonged to three AFT locals; and one year of my professional life was spent as PR director on the staff of one of the country's most militantly progressive unions.

But let's forget details such as this, and accept that effective ed tech-based instructional strategies do, in fact, prove cost-effective. Let's also forget, for the moment, the difficulty in obtaining the acceptance by teachers and their bargaining entities of any meaningful integration of ITV in the classroom instructional program. Having done this, we can then ask why is it that our arguments about cost-effectiveness have fallen on deaf ears in our attempts to impress school superintendents and school board members—people who, in a time of stratospherically increasing school costs, should be most eager to pounce on anything which promises to effect cash savings? To what degree is their failure to be convinced a function of our having failed to point out that while effective use of ITV might save many millions over the next decade or so, that for the *next year*—the major concern of most superintendents—the tool-up effort in terms of capital and released time expenditures will not reduce costs, but actually increase them. How does a superintendent who finds himself or herself, say, $4,000,000 in the hole for that next year (because that's what his teachers union is demanding in salary increases) say "yes" on the four million to ITV, and "no" to the union?

But let's go even further and forget any futurecasting and long-range theorizing about what can (or, more accurately, *cannot*) be done tomorrow, and come back to today: a "today" which, I cannot stress too strongly, is 30 years into television, more than 50 into radio, and 75 to 100 into film and audio recording; in other words, a today where in speaking of the media, the future is already *now*!

How do those who argue a viable future for TV in formal education explain away the fact that a quarter-century after Buffalo Bob and Uncle Miltie, and a score of years after Lucy peaked, a recent government survey could show that 25 percent of our schools have not a single TV set, and another 50 percent have fewer than five. (Thirteen percent have five to nine; 12 percent, 10 or more.) From all of which we can extrapolate that five to seven percent of the nation's classrooms are receiver-equipped.

Even more difficult, how, in light of these figures, and the facts about ITFS stated at the outset, do those who make the claim argue that ITV is viable and significant today? I find it interesting that those who do so never give that one figure which would make or break their case: the percentage of the K-12 enrollment who regularly—and we could define "regularly" as liberally as something like once or twice a week—receive instruction in at least one subject area via TV. Or, let's ask it this way: What are the odds that at a given moment, a student will find himself or herself seated in a classroom where (1) there is a TV set; (2) on which can be received an ITV lesson at his or her grade level; (3) in the subject he or she's studying at that time; (4) said class being staffed by a teacher willing to turn on the set?

Do we sometimes confuse the amount of ITV sent out over the air (accounting for some 33 percent of all Public Television transmissions), with the amounts actually tuned into and used? (And once again, I'd reiterate my earlier point about ITFS—that if ITV were of any significance, schools would not accept only one channel of service at a time.)

A possible reason why many of us in Public TV may be in this state of confusion lies in the role that instructional television has historically played in the development and financing of the medium. Almost one-half of all Public TV stations are licensed to state ETV commissions or to public school systems—and for these ITV was and is their *raison d'etre*. For the community stations—one-quarter of the total, including almost all of the largest—ITV has been for them what Proctor and Gamble has traditionally been for commercial TV: the single largest source of revenue. The overhead which community stations realize from the head tax paid by school systems subscribing to their ITV services still pays a major part of their non-schooltime programming costs. It is interesting to note, however, that as new sources of revenue are derived by PTV (e.g., CPB station grants and viewer subscriptions), a number of stations, most notably WTTW, the Chicago Public outlet, are dropping ITV entirely.

A figure frequently quoted to refute contentions such as these as to the paucity of ITV usage within schools comes out of a study done several years back on school use of "Electric Company." How does one arguing my position explain, as some read that study to state, that 40 percent of early elementary grade children are watching that series in class? To which the answer is, 40 percent don't! What that still all-too-frequently misread and misquoted study reported was that in 40 percent of those schools which can receive TV(?), *some* use of "Electric Company" was indicated. Thus, if a school had a total of, say, nine second through fourth grade classes—which, given "Electric Company's" 130 shows per season means a potential of 1170 (9 x 130 = 1170) classroom usage days—and if one or more teachers reported one or more days of use out of the possible 1170, then that whole school was included in the 40 percent.

Reference to "Electric Company" brings up its Children's Television Workshop companion series, "Sesame Street," which, in turn, leads me to some of the positive directions in which I think TV as an instructional medium may be heading.

One of the major reasons that "Sesame" is such a solid success is precisely because it is *not* an in-school ITV series: because it aims at a non-school attending, pre-school audience, there are no teachers acting as gatekeepers to prevent children from watching it.

Thus, taking the cue from "Sesame," if TV is to be the offeror of effective, objective-specified instruction, it will not come about as a function of programming designed for use in schools where it never will be used—but through programming like "Sesame Street" which is broadcast in after-school and weekend kidtime hours.

Even if such programming reaches relatively small percentages of youngsters—and as "Sesame Street" shows, this certainly need not be the case—small percentages of large, nationwide audiences still mean many millions reached. (Numbers certainly many times larger than those reached in schools by ITV.)

In other words, if I am correct in writing off school television as an instructional medium, home-viewed TV will increasingly play this role. But that only means *the schools* will be getting along without us.

Not the kids!

10.

Instructional Television, Interaction and Learning Objectives

Richard W. Burns

Any discussion of learning eventually involves the consideration of many variables, ranging from the nature of the learner through the gamut of content, materials, setting, time and means to the specifying of terminal objectives. Accompanying these variables are multiple constraints involving, to name a few, legal parameters, administrative policies, economic resources, parental concerns, local mores and individual personalities. Thus, given all the factors operative in learning plus the lack of knowledge about instructional television (ITV), it is extremely difficult to generalize about either learner interaction with television as the means, or the types of objectives best adapted to a television medium. However, recognizing that progress is always a combination of trial and error, the following considerations are presented more to raise problems, stimulate thinking and suggest needed research than to delineate final conclusions applicable to ITV.

Considering the attributes of television as a medium, the first question to consider is, "Are there learning objectives which are peculiarly adapted to ITV?" Even though numerous reports have been made concerning the lack of statistically significant differences between media, i.e., print, non-print, audio, visual, audio-visual, etc., and perhaps the general conclusion reached that all objectives can be accomplished by *any* medium, these types of

Richard W. Burns is Professor of Education, University of Texas, El Paso.

studies beg two real issues. The first issue concerns the use to which the medium is put. If media are used exclusively or primarily as means of presenting information, then it is quite likely true that one medium is as functional as another, although some differences will exist. However, if the learner is to interact with the methods and materials to achieve specified performances, as in ITV, then media may have attributes which will demonstrate significant differences showing superiority in given instances of learning.

The second issue of concern to the major question of objectives in relation to media is efficiency. This is to say that even though two media presentations may accomplish the same objective, one may do it more efficiently, i.e., in less time, at lower cost or result in a greater proportion of learner successes. Research designs incorporating field studies of functional learning settings need to be made to determine the relevance of both of these issues. It must be understood that proponents of ITV are not claiming and never have claimed that television and associated technology are a cure-all for the educational weaknesses of our present educational system. In the long run one will, in all probability, find television fulfilling a significant but minor role in the total educational effort in the United States. One factor alone, cost, will restrict the full development and use of television to selected learning situations to which it is peculiarly adapted. For example, ITV may be used when the learning audience is extremely large or where the audience is geographically remote.

Getting to the heart of the first question, the following types or categories of objectives theoretically should fit ITV in some more unique way than another distinctly different medium:

1. An obvious first type of objective is one dealing with motion. In one sense this large category can be conceptually viewed as being composed of sub-categories relating to:

(a)   change (as in position);

(b)   development;

(c)   growth;

(d)   acceleration-deceleration;

(e)   assembly and disassembly processes and processes involving actions such as brushing, shading, drawing,
tracing, etc.; and

(f)   multiple but related movements, such as those involving
objects of the solar system.

A direct approach to achieving performance objectives involving
motion should be inherent in silent film, sound film, video with
and without sound and other similar formats. The efficiency
which can be achieved in controlling media attributes is in fact a
distinguishing characteristic of ITV. Examples of media attributes
relating to television presentations involve effective control and
use of such elements as color, animation, light, shading and speed
of transmission. An even more specific example can be indicated
by the effective control and use of presentation rate as in high
speed, low speed, time-lapse or hold presentations purposefully
designed to achieve a specialized concept, as in "how do seeds
germinate?"

2. A second category of objectives which should be a
"natural" for ITV are those involving concepts and related
performances whose achievement (learning) would be enhanced by
what might be called simultaneous presentations. Examples of
simultaneous presentations would involve such things as presenting
digital and iconic objects together, split screen presentations of
two simultaneous but separated actions, and audio and visual
stimuli. An illustration here could be a situation involving the
learner's development of a complex iconic reading skill, as in map
reading, where the "understanding" of the relationship of the
parts to the whole would be enhanced by either an audio or visual
presentation of "explanatory text." In this example, efficiency
might be enhanced by color coding; focusing to exclusion of
non-relevant detail; refocusing to include larger amounts of detail;
shifting of focus to different areas for reading; and tracing routes,
lines or connections on the map while at the same time presenting
a verbal explanation of relevant information. The nature of film,

as in video, and associated technology makes possible almost instantaneous control over the iconic sign object (in this example, the map).

3. A third area of potential superiority for television is in the formation of "3-D, thing" concepts where the "thing" cannot be directly viewed. One flat picture of the "thing" or even multiple pictures do not do justice to all of the dimensional aspects, as inside, outside, front, side, back and other views which may be better presented by film or video technology. As in prior examples, the associated technology of television can, in this case, be employed to enhance efficient learning. For example, color, black and white, inserted schematic diagrams, long range, wide range, close up and other possible techniques can all be integrated so that an "instructionalized" format is produced.

The above three categories are offered as examples where television may prove to have a unique advantage as a medium in the achievement of specified objectives. Although we have dealt with only one aspect of the relationship of objectives to ITV, it should be noted that:

- ITV may also be, when not superior to, equally as effective as other media in the achievement of other types of objectives.
- ITV may also be the medium of choice when other media are equally as effective if one considers pragmatic elements not generally treated as relevant to learning, such as teacher preference, ease of handling, convenience, retrievability, etc.

A related topic which should be mentioned is objectives which are "hard to describe in performance terms"—i.e., affective objectives and their attainment with ITV designs. Given our modern setting and contrast between attractive TV and dull (if not downright boring) textbooks, one needs to consider the attitude, interest and appreciation outcomes of media presentations.

A second major consideration is the relationship of ITV to the interactive process of learning. Learning (that name given to the process by which change comes about as detected by observing an individual's performance) occurs, from an Interactive Behaviorist's viewpoint, to the degree that each individual learner interacts with the process elements; namely, methods and materials. If the individual achieves (performs in a manner judged as meeting the criteria and conditions as specified in performance objectives) then, by definition, interaction has occurred and has been effective. If the learner does not achieve, then, by definition, the interaction did not occur or was not effective. Interaction is always a unique consequence of the interrelationships between learner variables, media variables and environmental variables. The number of interrelationships and their effects increases rapidly as the number of variables increases. Considering only two sets (learner and media) with from three to five variables in each set, a chart of the interactions which are possible is shown in Figure 1. For example, considering three variables in each set, learner and media, for a total of six, the number of unidirectional and bidirectional relationships which are possible between sets are given in columns 4 and 5. Columns 6 and 7 indicate the number of unidirectional and bidirectional relationships within and between set members. One must consider the bidirectional nature of some variables, since the particular nature of a variable may be such that under one set of conditions it will assist learning but in another set of conditions it may detract from learning. For example, in visual learning the number of cues provided may increase the probability of interaction toward specified objectives, or the addition of cues may interfere or distract from learning. This facilitation or inhibition depends on other factors, such as age of learner, visual reading skill or task to be performed.

The point being made here is that ITV differs from TV or ETV to the degree that *the variables of learning are purposefully arranged to secure maximum learning outcomes.* At our present state of knowledge we may not know enough about the nature of each variable which affects interaction, the number of variables taking part in the interaction nor the effects of each variable in the

Figure 1

Number of Possible Unidirectional and Bidirectional Relationships Between Variables of Two Sets

1	2	3	4	5	6	7
			$N_1(N_2)$	$2(N_1)(N_2)$	$\frac{N(N-1)}{2}$	$N(N-1)$
N_1	N_2	N	UD-S	BD-S	UD WS	BD WS
3	3	6	9	18	15	30
3	4	7	12	24	21	42
4	4	8	16	32	28	56
4	5	9	20	40	36	72
5	5	10	25	50	45	90

N_1 = No. of learner variables
N_2 = No. of media variables
N = Total No. of variables
UD = Unidirectional

BD = Bidirectional
S = Between sets
W = Within sets

interactive process. (That these variables are presently being assessed in ITV evaluation designs is clarified by Williams and Stanford in their chapter in this book.) One immediate need is to relentlessly pursue, in the hope of determining, the contributions that each learning variable makes to a given learning situation so that the tremendous cost of ITV will prove cost-effective.

It is beyond the scope of this chapter to either detail all the learning variables or elaborate what is presently known concerning selected variables and their role in interaction. However, Figure 2 presents a representative listing of variables for consideration. In each of the three categories, 10 variables are listed, some of them quite general, which are illustrative of the types of things needed to be studied in interrelated process settings.

As a last consideration, the need to view any learning situation or segment thereof in relation to its being a systematic endeavor should be mentioned. In reality, as indicated at the beginning of this chapter, there are not only learner, process and immediate environmental variables but also social, cultural and political realities to face. That is, to devise a functional learning strategy those involved need to know the objectives of the strategy as based on the total operational circumstances. In essence this means that a set of criteria should be identified as parameters and guidelines to be followed in devising the details of the strategy for learning. Without criteria the result is often a fragmented series of efforts, each segment only efficient unto itself, but sadly lacking qualities necessary to the concept of "total education of the learner." Although ITV will only be one facet of this whole, attention needs to be paid to how ITV can most effectively contribute to learning, broadly conceived. Any given set of criteria may differ from one school to another, considering the tasks to be achieved.

It is doubtful that anyone could finalize a list of all the criteria which might be considered in the development of a comprehensive strategy but the following 25 factors are worthy of consideration. Again, it is beyond the scope of the present chapter

Figure 2

*Representative Variables for the Three
Major Categories Affecting Interaction*

Learner Variables

1. reading level
2. reading rate
3. vocabulary literacy
4. general learning rate
5. I.Q.
6. mathematical reasoning
7. special aptitudes
8. personality characteristics
9. listening comprehension
10. prior related achievement
11. etc.

Media Variables

1. form of encoding
2. duration of stimulus
3. response demand type
4. frequency of response
5. step size
6. type of feedback
7. amount of feedback information
8. numbers of cues
9. type of cues
10. color vs. black-and-white
11. etc.

Environmental Variables

1. audience size
2. room size
3. freedom from interfering stimuli
4. accessibility of resource materials
5. general learning atmosphere (i.e., pleasant, relaxed)
6. presence-absence of instructor
7. lighting
8. temperature
9. acoustic qualities
10. visual quality
11. etc.

to consider all the ramifications and implications of each factor. It is quite likely that all 25 factors are not present in any single segment of learning, but the presence or absence of any factor should be *purposeful* rather than a result of faulty planning. No hierarchy of importance is intended in the order of the presentation which follows.

1. *Specification of performance objectives.* This topic is extensively treated in the literature and should be obviously significant.

2. *Prerequisite skills.* Often these are assumed, as for example, the learner's reading level. Special skills, however, may need special consideration as measured by a pretest of prerequisite skills.

3. *Frame of reference.* This is useful to assist at entry and to maintain an integrated whole during the learning process.

4. *Focus.* Attending is a necessary factor, not merely at the start, but throughout the learning process.

5. *Entry Level.* Here one must consider factors other than specific prerequisite skills, such as age, grade, maturity and personality characteristics.

6. *Pretest of objectives.* This element considers that it is a waste of time for learners to participate in the acquiring of performance already in their repertoire of behavior. A pretest of this type allows the learner to proceed with relevant learning.

7. *Media or methods and materials fit the objectives.* This element considers the relationship between objectives involving concept formation, translating, concluding, memorizing, motion, etc., and the sensory input of media such as visual object, pictorial object, verbal, motion, etc.

8. *Media attributes.* This factor considers elements other than those in (7) above, such as color, number of cues, types of cues, simultaneous presentation of audio plus visual, time of stimulus exposure, retrievability, etc.

9. *Learning alternatives.* This factor is based on the premise that all learners will not respond to one given strategy, and

therefore learning in terms of *S*'s successes is enhanced by providing alternative methods. Examples would be offered by on-the-job training, reading, laboratory, discussion, programmed instruction, motion pictures, CAI, etc.

10. *Type of response.* Consideration is given to not only the overt-covert dichotomy but also to whether the response called for is exact reproduction, original expression, concept formation, recognition, approximate recall, etc. Learning interactions should be directed toward and fit the final performances required.

11. *Presentation rate.* This entails the rate of concept formation, reading rate, listening rate as well as use of special techniques, such as fast and slow motion.

12. *Feedback.* A consideration of its presence or absence, type of feedback, amount of information supplied and time of feedback (immediate or delayed).

13. *Step size.* Consideration of amount of information or complexity of problem or concept, length of segments between check points (feedback), length of time between responses, contribution of the learning segment to the terminal objective (part-whole relationship) and time span between correct responses.

14. *Sequencing.* This refers to whether the parts of a given learning segment or the segments themselves are extrinsically arranged (instructor or media demand a sequence) or intrinsically arranged (learner selects stimuli elements to respond to in any order he pleases).

15. *Maintenance.* This is an often neglected consideration when learning segments are independently developed, in which case each segment can be claimed efficient and functional yet the whole may fall short of expectations. This concept refers to the requirement in subsequent learning segments of the use of information and skills learned in prior segments. It has often been said that the one sure thing that transpires in education is forgetting.

16. *Review.* This is a different concept than Maintenance (No. 15 above) or Summary (No. 17 below) although the three

factors may be related. The two crucial decisions here are whether to provide it or not and, if so, whether the review (learn again, study again, look at anew, look back at) should be in the original or in a different context.

17. *Summary*. The instructor brings together in concise form the main elements. This is probably related to "short" and "long term" memory concepts or to information storage and retrieval.

18. *Time*. As used here, this refers to whether the learner is allowed to go at his own pace and whether he may take as much time as needed to reach performance criteria.

19. *Communication skills*. Since reading, listening, speaking, writing, vocabulary literacy and other related aspects are important in learning, it appears that the development of these skills should be part of all aspects and segments of learning. Each segment of learning must stress and be responsible for technical terms, special reading skills and the communication of ideas relevant to what is being learned.

20. *Integration*. Everyone "kind of" talks about this but little is actually done about it. The obvious idea is to integrate knowledge (in the broad sense of the term) as, for example, relating the study of history to food, medicine, economics, anthropology, language, culture, archeology, political science, science, etc.

21. *Application and use*. Although this factor is related to maintenance and other elements, the point here is to emphasize that this feature of learning is, in the final analysis, what learning ultimately entails. However, much of what is learned in school appears to have little, and sometimes no, relationship to real life after school. Each learning segment should require the learner to apply and use, in as functional a context as possible, that which is being learned.

22. *Recycling*. This feature in learning considers the possibility that all learners will not achieve performance criteria with an initial effort but may need to spend more time, and interact in other ways, i.e., recycle or try again.

23. *Formative Evaluation.* Formative evaluation plays several roles in ITV, as in development and evaluation of whole program (system) success, in development and evaluation of program segments and as an integral part of any process segment for learners in terms of the learner receiving information about learning success. In this sense, formative evaluation, as contrasted with summative evaluation, plays a role in developmental stages, whether we are talking about program development or the educational development of the learner.

24. *Summative Evaluation.* Summative measures are either designed to assess the achievement of program and system objectives or learner achievement of learning objectives. The latter type is complicated in practice because of the issue developing over the use of norm-referenced testing (NRT) or criterion-referenced testing (CRT) as the appropriate type of summative measuring device to employ as a final assessment.

25. *Value Development.* This element suggests that all cognitive and psychomotor objectives are automatically and unavoidably accompanied by affective types of learning as interests, attitudes and appreciations. This is another way of saying that affective objectives, in this instance specifically values, are accomplished (learned) as students interact in learning environments achieving cognitive and psychomotor performances. No learning segment can be presented or taught in mathematics, science, language or any other area in isolation from the learner's emotional or feeling domain. Thus, every cognitive and psychomotor learning segment must recognize that all its parts and aspects are serving as learning elements for affective ends and should be purposefully designed with this realization in mind.

In summary, what has been said is simply that ITV must:

a. discover and implement learning segments the objectives of which are uniquely adapted to ITV;

b. manipulate its unique attributes to produce learner interaction and thus achieve efficiency; and

c. recognize that it is but a part of a total education effort and as such must be realistically cognizant of criteria or factors pertaining to the whole. Examples or elements of each of these three considerations have been given for further consideration.

11.

In-School Television and the New Technology

Rudy Bretz

What happened to in-school television? While not exactly commonplace today, it certainly is no longer news, either to the
newspapers or to the professional journals. The belief has
developed that in-school television has withered or died. My own
personal experience gives me a contrary view. After repeatedly
running into elaborate and heavily used television systems of
various kinds at schools and training centers, I am pursuaded that
in-school television is alive and well.

We lack recent data, but a survey of public schools made by
the HEW in 1970 gives support to my view. It was revealed in this
study that 90 percent of large-city elementary schools had TV
receivers and made use of educational or instructional telecasts,
and that nationally well over half of all schools used television.

Here is some more information that the HEW school staffing
survey revealed.

- Over six and one-half million pupils attended schools
  that each had 10 or more TV receivers available for
  classroom use.
- Over half of the secondary schools in suburban areas
  had videotape recorders.
- Eight percent of the elementary schools and 14 percent

Rudy Bretz is a consultant to The Rand Corporation, Santa Monica,
California.

of the secondary schools had some kind of closed-circuit TV in operation, from a single camera with videotape recorder to a full-fledged ITFS distribution system and central studios. This amounted to over 7000 schools.

• In general it was concluded in this study that 75 percent of all public schools used television in some way, or at least had the equipment to do so; for what it may mean, 33 million pupils were enrolled in those schools.

If this were current data it would hardly warrant an obituary for instructional TV in general or in-school TV specifically. But it is six or seven years old. Since that time many technological advances have been made that greatly *increase* the availability and usefulness of TV in education and training. The current level of use must be considerably higher in every area.

At the same time, thinking in education has been changing its direction. The great body of research in the early years, generated seemingly in the hopes of finding some magical quality of the television medium itself that was independent of content and teaching strategy, came up with the unanimous but dissapointing verdict: no significant difference. It is easy now in hindsight to say, "well, why *should* there have been any difference?" It was still the same lock-step instruction—presentation of information—with learning measured by the same tests. Mainly because objective tests were used, it was only *cognitive* learning that was being investigated. Instruction in skills was considered inappropriate to television, or beyond its capabilities. The achievement of affective objectives was considered totally beyond measurement. Promoted by creative producers to justify artistic production, affective objectives were often rejected (or at least neglected) by educators because they made no measurable difference on the cognitive tests, they cost extra money and they appeared to add an incongruous and distracting entertainment element in what should be serious learning. (In some cases, of course, they probably did.)

The grants dwindled and the researchers and the theorists lost interest in television. Today the thrust is more in the direction of individualization, and the encountering of concepts through personal *discovery* rather than *presentation*. Educators today emphasize the role of the learner in managing his own instruction, putting greater responsibilities on him to apply his own strategies, within the range of choice allowed by the facilities and materials at his disposal; and thus not only learning, but learning how to learn at the same time.

The new approach reduces the role of lesson presentation in the group mode, and tends to emphasize other teacher activities. Interestingly the technology of television has now become better adapted for use in these *other* instructional activities, such as skills learning, and can be used in the *individual mode* as never before. For example, one of the most common uses of television in schools today is to record on videotape and play back the performance of individuals and groups that are learning skills of various kinds. Thus, thanks to technological changes, such as those described below, in-school television is becoming far different from the "instructional TV" that was researched so widely some two decades ago. The technology has vaulted ahead of the research "conclusions."

Cameras

Twenty years ago only the huge standard broadcast cameras were made, built around the Image Orthicon tube, and costing about $20,000 per camera. During the middle 1950s the smaller vidicon tube was developed, and this made small, low-cost TV cameras possible.

Now, a new family of vidicon tubes has taken over. Two-thirds the previous vidicon size both in diameter and length, these are comparable in price, but their small size and thus flexibility of use is so important that they have quickly replaced previous vidicons.

Television cameras as small as photographic cameras, plus videotape recorders you can carry, give television almost the same flexibility as cinematography. With "portapak" equipment, a cameraman can now go anywhere, camera in hand and VTR slung on a strap over his shoulder, all of it battery-operated. The microphone is built into the camera.

The solid state revolution has swept through the world of electronics, and vacuum tubes everywhere have been replaced with transisters, and transisters in turn by integrated circuits. By the early 1970s the last remaining vacuum tube in any TV camera was the picture tube itself. Today even this is threatened by the Charge Coupled Device (CCD), a picture pickup device made of several small wafers; prototype CCD cameras are smaller than anything yet produced—close to the size of a two-inch cube—but these will remain essentially in the laboratory for the next few years.

The increased flexibility and ease of handling brought about by the electronics revolution have enabled schools to use television equipment in ways hardly dreamed of in the early 1950s.

The Videotape Recorder

This year videotape is 20 years old. The current broadcast standards are close relatives of the original Ampex four-head "quadraplex" system which recorded some 50 tracks to the inch, crosswise on two-inch-wide tape. Four or five years later, a second videotape principle, helical scanning, made its appearance—and opened the door to video origination and flexible scheduling of TV use by the schools.

In this method of recording, successive tracks are recorded in a long slant across the tape, making it possible to put an entire video field or frame on each line. When, in playing back, the forward motion of the tape is stopped, the machine scans the same frame repeatedly, displaying a still image. If the forward speed is less than normal, some tracks are scanned more than once, and the result is slow motion. While not technically perfect, this feature was highly instrumental in suiting the helical-scan VTR for an instructional function which had never really been fulfilled before: self-observation. Some believe that more videotape recorders were acquired and used by schools for this purpose than for any other. The 1970 HEW survey revealed that one out of every four public schools had videotape recorders—that amounts to 20,000 schools, both elementary and secondary. For secondary schools alone the ratio is one in three. If self-observation is not the major use for this equipment, it is certainly high on the list. Coaches can critique sports performances for the players, individuals can study their skill techniques in everything from archery to typing, including public speaking effectiveness. While this had been possible with film for many years, it was rarely done, mainly because of the cost, but also because of the long delay between shooting and screening which precluded immediate feedback.

The first helical-scan machines used two-inch-wide tape, but soon VTRs were accomplishing nearly the same result with tape of one-inch and ½-inch width, at considerable cost savings, especially if the tapes were to be archived. One manufacturer, Akai of Japan, developed a very successful system, now with acceptable quality color, utilizing tape of ¼-inch width.

In 1972 Sony introduced a ¾-inch tape, in 10 to 60 minute lengths, totally enclosed in a cassette. One merely inserts the cassette, just as he would an audiotape cassette, and presses the "play" (or the "record") button. Even young pupils can operate the equipment satisfactorily.

As the market has grown, mass production and rapid new development have followed, bringing the prices of the ever smaller machines down toward the cost of audiotape recorders. In the early 60s, when helical-scan machines were enjoying their first big acceptance, the best helical-scan VTR, using one-inch tape, cost around $12,000. Today the same quality can be obtained from a machine costing about one-tenth that price.

Furthermore, the greatest drawback to helical-scan VTRs, their low reliability, and hence high cost of maintenance, is virtually a thing of the past. The modern machines, equal in quality to top-of-the-line models a dozen years ago, have been called "one hundred times more reliable."*

The Videodisc

Now we are on the brink of another revolution—the introduction of the videodisc. The great advantage of this new technology will be economic. While videodisc playback equipment will be more expensive than film, it will be considerably under the present costs of ¾-inch VTRs. The greatest saving, however, will be in the cost of discs as contrasted with videotape reels or videotape cassettes.

Comparative cost estimates of videodisc distribution, versus film and videotape, indicate that a half-hour motion-visual program on disc will cost about 1/30 as much as ¾-inch videotape and 1/100 as much as 16mm film. (See the chapter by E.W. Schneider, in this book.) This per-copy estimate is based on the distribution of 1000 copies of a given program. However, to make a *single recording* on videodisc, without copies (e.g., for self-observation) will cost almost twice as much as 8mm film and six times as much as ¾-inch videotape.

Thus videodiscs, at least for the immediate future, will *not* be a medium for local recording. Videodisc *recorders* are not being readied for the general market today, only disc *playback* equipment. Educators who want to make their own recordings will continue to use helical-scan videotape. Discs will be centrally produced and distributed in large quantity just as instructional films, published materials and many videotapes are today—but at a much lower cost per student.

In the early stages of any new technology, reliability and standardization problems are to be expected. The low cost of widely distributed software, however, may quickly overcome these drawbacks if the "chicken-and-egg" problem can be overcome.

*K. Winslow. Video Systems: Photomethods Progress Report. *Photomethods*, November 1974, 42.

That is, low-cost software can only be possible when playback machines are widespread, and people won't buy the playback equipment until the software that they want to use is available at low cost. How long videodiscs can hold the limelight is another question. Sony's video *card*, a flexible two inches by eight inches in size, is *already* "waiting in the wings."

The Distribution of
Prerecorded Programs

During the last decade the appearance of increasingly easier-to-acquire and easier-to-operate videotape equipment has opened up many possibilities for distribution of prerecorded materials directly to the school. This trend has far from run its course; we are probably only at the beginning of a line of development that will not end until audio-video origination, distribution and display equipment have passed through the present institutional phase and become as available to individuals as high quality audio and photographic equipment is today, and as commonplace in the consumer market.

One path in this direction involves off-the-air videotape recording at the school, for the purpose of: (1) delaying a program so it may be played back at a more convenient time; (2) playing a program back many times at the convenience of many classes; or (3) accumulating a library of tapes for present and future use. If the demand is not great, any one of these things can be done by simply carrying the videotape player into the classroom when a tape is requested. When the load is heavier, schools operate more efficiently with a central recording and playback location in the school, distributing over an internal, intra-school wired network to the classrooms.

Some schools use a method of distribution which involves the broadcast of tapes after regular station hours to unattended VTRs at the schools. Before a given tape is run, a coded series of pulses automatically rolls the recorders at all schools that have requested it. When the school AV men return in the morning, they find their tapes for the day waiting for them.

Instructional Broadcasting Facilities
and Cable Television

In addition to technological improvements in hardware (cameras and recorders) and software (videotape and discs), in-school television has changed and is continuing to change due to the growth of instructional broadcasting and cable TV facilities.

When the FCC reserved educational television channels in the early 1950s, it was told to expect a demand for a tenth of all TV channels within a few years. Educators and communities were slow to organize, however, and it was more than 10 years before one out of every 10 operating TV stations was a non-commercial station. In the last 13 years, however, while commercial television continued to grow, non-commercial TV grew faster. Today one out of every three or four television stations in this country is an "educational" station, a far greater proportion than even its enthusiastic proponents originally expected. There were, at the beginning of 1976, 259 non-commercial television stations in operation. Fourteen communities supported two such stations each, and three cities, New York, Miami and Los Angeles, each had three.

Since almost all of these carry *instructional* programs during *school hours*, it can be safely said that the nationwide total of *instructional* broadcasts, per day, week or month, has more than doubled in the last decade.

There has been a strong trend away from insistence on locally produced lessons toward an acceptance of regionally or nationally distributed programs. The first step was taken in the 1950s and 1960s when at least 22 state networks were established to share programs between ETV stations within the state. Now these have been consolidated into six regional networks. Distribution is sometimes live, more often with videotape. Independent instructional tape libraries are flourishing. As a result there are more well-conceived and well-produced programs used in the schools than was ever possible in the days of strict local autonomy.

Cable television systems have multiplied at about the same

rate as the non-commercial broadcasting stations, doubling during the last 10 years to over 3300 today. The total number of subscribers, however, has practically exploded, climbing from 1.5 million in 1966 to almost nine million today, an increase of nearly 600 percent.

As far as instruction is concerned, however, cable apparently remains far more a *potential* means than an active one. A prime characteristic of cable, its relative abundance of channels, does not, *so far* at least, apply to instruction. But one should watch for changes here as cable TV continues to expand throughout the nation.

Summary

This brief synopsis of recent technical advances has reported on:

- the appearance of steadily smaller, less expensive, more reliable and better quality camera, VTR and associated equipment;
- the promise of further development along each of these directions, mostly through improvements in existing kinds of equipment, but also through the introduction of new technology, such as the videodisc and the videocard;
- a steady growth in non-commercial, educational, public broadcasting stations (call them what you will) that has not yet begun to level off; and
- a slow, but potentially promising, in-school utilization of cable TV.

12.

Videodiscs, or the Individualization of Instructional Television

E.W. Schneider

There are almost as many reasons to explain the disappointingly slow development of instructional television as there are to explain crime on city streets. Within the next year, a few of the classic "buts" directed at instructional television are going to be much less compelling. By June, 1977, *videodiscs* will be widely available in the United States.

Already, videodiscs have been brought to market in West Germany and in the United Kingdom. Several companies are gearing up now to introduce videodisc technology to the American public. They are developing rival playback machines that sense the disc's video information in different ways. Teldec and RCA players have transducers that must maintain mechanical contact with a spinning disc; MCA and Philips (Norelco) have joined forces to market a player that uses a light beam and a photo-diode. The mechanical players will be less expensive, but their discs will wear out much sooner, and they will not allow the user to move around in the instructional materials, speeding forward or backward or even freezing the action for a closer, longer look. These limitations will be mildly annoying to the home user, but they will become intolerable to the modern educator, if he has the opportunity to work with the optical videodisc. To see why, let's explore the optical approach in greater detail.

E.W. Schneider is with the Institute for Computer Uses in Education, Brigham Young University, Provo, Utah.

A prototype of a videodisc player intended for home use is shown in Figure 1. Basically, the unit consists of a turntable (Figure 2) scanned by a sliding carriage. A microscope objective mounted on the carriage focuses the light from a low-power laser on the reflective surface of the videodisc. A track of microscopic pits or bumps of varying lengths has been pressed into the plastic surface of the disc (Figure 3). If the laser light shines on a portion of the disc where there is no pit, the light is reflected back along the same optical path and is detected by a photo-receptor. If the light shines into a pit, it is diffused, and very little light returns along the original path. The transition points from pit to no pit, and vice versa, define the zero-crossings of the original frequency-modulated video signal. Using the zero crossing information, the original composite video waveform is reconstructed, and is used to modulate an appropriate VHF carrier so that the signal may be input to the antenna terminals of a conventional television receiver.

Each disc can play up to 30 minutes of video material using just one side of the disc. With each revolution, one frame of video is displayed; the track width for each frame, pits and guard-bands included, is approximately two microns wide. In order to keep eccentricities in the replicated disc and other such perturbations from making the laser beam miss the track of pits, a servo-system controls a galvanometer mirror, which keeps the laser beam centered on the desired track. By stepping the mirror motor, it is possible to access any one of several adjacent tracks; access to more distant tracks requires movement of the entire carriage. This is accomplished with a conventional electric motor and lead-screw arrangement. If the galvanometer mirror is stepped backward one track during each retrace cycle, the same frame is played over and over again, providing a "freeze frame" capability. If every track is played twice, a slow-motion effect is obtained. All kinds of tinkering are possible, because each frame has a digital address which is read by the player; in fact, during the fast forward and fast reverse operations, the frame address is superimposed on a

Figure 1

Prototype of Philips/MCA Videodisc Player Unit

Prototype of Philips/MCA videodisc player unit. (Courtesy of MCA Disco-Vision, Inc.)

Figure 2

Optical Videodisc Playback System

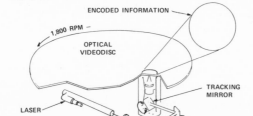

Schematic view of videodisc playback system. The light beam from a helium-neon gas laser is focused on the surface of the disc. Modulated light, reflected from the disc, passes back along the same path to the beam splitter, where it separates and goes to the photo-detector. Electronic signal processing reconstructs the video signal. Servo-systems control the tracking mirror and the focusing lens to keep the beam "on target." (Courtesy of MCA Disco-Vision, Inc.)

Figure 3

Surface of Videodisc as Seen with Electron Microscope

Electron micrograph of replicated videodisc (magnified approximately 22,000 times). Like well-regimented mountain ranges, three tracks of "information bumps" rise from the flat surface of the disc. (Courtesy of MCA Disco-Vision, Inc.)

small portion of the screen. If we add a small microprocessor and give it access to the frame number register and also let it control the track selection process. . . but, I am getting ahead of my story; I have just barely described the machine and already I am modifying it. To summarize its hardware advantages, we can say that optical videodiscs are free of the wear factors characteristic of videotape players, provide very high density of information storage, and, compared with the prior art, are delightfully easy on the pocketbook; a player will cost about $500.00, and discs should cost about $2.00 to $5.00 each, depending upon program material.

Economics of Videodiscs

There are several cost comparisons that I would like to share with you. These data were assembled with the help of Eddy Zwaneveld of BYU's Motion Picture Studio. Table 1 shows the

Table 1

Typical Costs of A V Reproduction Equipment

1.	8mm video player and monitor	$1,592.00
2.	¾" videotape cassette player and monitor	1,500.00
3.	Optical videodisc player and monitor	900.00
4.	16mm projector and screen	825.00
5.	8mm projector and screen	554.00

Table 2

*Per-copy Costs for a One-half
Hour Motion Visual Program*

Medium	Quantity			
	1	10	100	1000
16mm film	$417.00	$108.00	$84.52	$66.17
8mm film	285.00	66.00	52.00	44.76
¾" videocassette	70.00	31.00	21.25	18.50
Videodisc	450.00	46.00	3.01	.63

relative costs of reproducing equipment. With each video system, I have included the costs of a color monitor. With each motion picture system, I have included the cost of a screen. As you can see, videodisc is the cheapest video apparatus, but it is not as inexpensive as a film projector.

The second cost comparison (Table 2) is more telling. Here, we have compared the per-copy cost for 1, 10, 100 and 1000 copies of a 30-minute program. We see that videodisc is not the cheapest for various small numbers of copies, but that its cost drops quite rapidly with any real volume. To combine these cost estimates, let us suppose that we have a cozy education network of one hundred elementary schools, in a two hundred square-mile area. We provide each school with the capability of viewing six different programs simultaneously, and we also provide each school with a library (or in the case of networks, a catalog) of two hundred 30-minute programs. Each program is shown an average of four times during each school year. In the case of centrally programmed systems, approximately 35 channels would be required, and each program would be played an average of three hundred times per year. If the initial outlay is amortized over five years, the yearly costs for the competing delivery systems are shown in Table 3. The recurring costs after the initial five-year period arise from the need to replace program copies that wear out, and maintenance requirements. We conclude that this network can save about $23,000.00 a year by giving each school its own library of videodiscs, instead of running even a conventional film distribution system. If the schools contemplate a closed-circuit TV system, they can reduce the average annual cost by 42 percent—if they install videodiscs instead of videotapes at their head-end studios.

Educational Uses of Videodiscs

Judging by the cost figures shown above, it will only be a matter of time until videodiscs completely replace conventional motion pictures in educational institutions. This is especially true

Table 3

Annual Costs (in thousands of dollars) for an Education Network (group viewing)

Medium	Year		
	1-5	6-10	total-10 year
Local Libraries			
¾" videotape	314.	48.	1,570.
16mm film	437.4	39.	2,382.
videodisc	168.	48.	1,080.
Networks			
Closed-circuit TV			
¾" videotapes at head-end	310.36	116.2	2,383.
videodiscs at head-end	247.8	96.	1,239.
16mm film—Lending Library	182.36	79.6	1,310.

if projection television displays become just a bit cheaper. It is important to realize that the economic advantage of videodiscs is due to their durability and ruggedness, as well as to their low purchase costs. In our film rental library, 50 bookings of one print is about all that we can expect before scratches and torn sprocket holes take their toll. Videotape cassettes are good for two- to three-hundred plays. With optical videodiscs, fingerprints, dust and surface scratches can't penetrate the plastic "sandwich" that protects the inner reflective surface. When the disc is played, its outer surface, dust, scratches and all, is outside the focal range of the microscope objective. The player can show the same frame, hour after hour, without any degradation of the television image.

Another and more innovative possibility is the use of videodiscs to replace the monochrome postcard reproductions that fine arts students buy, and the sets of microscope slides that are inflicted on students of medicine and life sciences. Table 4

Table 4

Per Frame Costs, in dollars,
for Still Visuals
(54,000 frames per set)

Medium	Quantity			
	1	10	100	1000
35mm color slides	0.25	0.20	0.15	0.09
35mm color filmstrips	0.122	0.02	0.0085	0.0085
microfiche, color	0.15	0.022	0.0083	0.0083
microfilm, monochrome	0.10	0.017	0.0076	0.0076
videodisc	0.0083	0.0009	0.00006	0.00001

compares the costs of color slides, filmstrips and microfiche to a videodisc designed to show still images (the frames are recorded on concentric circular tracks, instead of on a continuous helix). We conclude that, whenever a large number of images (more than 1800) is required, *nothing* is cheaper than videodisc.

Videodiscs would also replace the ubiquitous slide/tape shows. In order to provide audio, the videodisc would work in a normal "motion picture" manner when audio was required. When audio is not required, a still-frame or a sequence of still-frames could be shown. The still-frames would contain study questions, discussion points or summaries, and the video player would continue to show them until it received a command to go on.

More sophisticated interactive applications would require the addition of a more elaborate keyboard and a digital microprocessor to control the videodisc player. For example, it will be possible when studying dynamic systems, such as the growth of an embryo or the oscillations of a mechanical system, to record different views of the same process on adjacent videodisc tracks, and to switch from one viewpoint to another by pressing buttons on an external keyboard. This capability would allow the student to manipulate, at least in a crude way, the three-dimensional materials under study.

Interactive Instruction

We are in the initial design phases of specifying not one but a family of interactive machines that are capable, in varying degrees, of asking questions and responding to students' answers. The simplest machine would accept multiple choice answers (A, B, C, D) and would branch to a specific frame, depending upon which answer were selected. With the addition of a small amount of memory, such machines would work well in adaptive testing applications, where the selection of the next test item depends upon the response history of the student up to that point. A little more memory, say on the order of two to four thousand words, and a simple character generator to display about 50 characters of student input would allow the videodisc system to perform satisfactorily as a self-contained computer-assisted instruction (CAI) system. We will be able to get by with a very small memory because we will appropriate some of the video frames on the disc to store digital instructions and data for the microprocessor. Whenever such a digital frame is encountered, it will automatically load data into a specified region of the microprocessor's memory. With this approach, the program in memory only needs to interpret the student's next answer and display an appropriate videodisc frame in response. Branching to the next frame may cause a new program to be loaded, and it will interpret the subsequent response, etc. The response time on this system (the mean amount of time that a student must wait to see the next frame) should compare favorably with that of existing CAI systems, as long as the instructional materials can be packaged into fairly small, self-contained modules. If all of the frames for a given module are confined to a small region of the videodisc, the player's optics carriage will not have far to travel, and the response time will not be noticeable.

Figure 4

Block Diagram of a "Mindbender"
Interactive Videodisc System

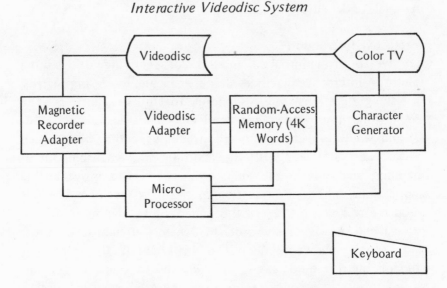

Our most elaborate system, the "Mindbender" system (Figure 4), will consist of a small color TV monitor, a videodisc, a keyboard, a microprocessor and some miscellaneous interconnection electronics. We estimate that a complete hardware system to deliver this kind of computer-assisted instruction would cost approximately $1,800.00. With the usual tack-ons for sales and service and for return on investment, the monthly rental charge to a student would be approximately $80.00. If three or four college students got together, they could easily afford to have their own terminal, and when they were tired of studying, it could play "Airport" or "Ben Hur" as well as picking up the "Johnny Carson Show." In order to keep the student's instructor and the University's registrar informed of his progress in the course, the individual lessons could be stamped out on much smaller five-minute videodiscs, that would have a magnetic band in the otherwise unused center. The student's identification number and the results of the test administered at the end of the lesson would be recorded on this band. The student would return the completed lesson disc to the school library, where the magnetic band would be read, the information would be fed to a central recordkeeping computer and the band would be erased for use by the next student. The computer would analyze test results, and compare them with previous test results. It would then prepare a summary of the student's performance with comments and recommendations that would be typed out at a remote printer in the library. The student files would also be analyzed by the student's instructor to determine both individual and group performance on the learning materials. This same technique would also work well for a correspondence school, because videodiscs are small, light and easy to mail.

Development Versus Delivery Systems

When used in this interactive fashion, videodiscs would require a clear distinction between the delivery system and the development system. This distinction has not been necessary in earlier CAI systems, because the instructional content was always stored in a modifiable medium, usually magnetic tape or disc. When instructional content is pressed rapidly and firmly into soft plastic, it is no longer possible to correct misspelled words, or to fix misleading feedback messages. A completely separate system that uses easily modifiable storage must be used to develop, evaluate and revise instructional content. This development system will, in all probability, resemble existing CAI systems rather closely, with the addition of hardware to produce a videodisc master that will be used to press the videodiscs.

Prerequisites for Successful Videodisc Instructional Systems

Implementing these kinds of systems will not be a matter of simply waiting for the hardware. The major feasibility questions do not revolve around the videodisc technology, but around a still-infant *instructional* technology. To be really cost-effective, videodiscs must be stamped in reasonable numbers; and, therefore, a reasonable number of schools and students must agree to use them. This acceptance will not occur unless the material stamped on the disc really works, and works well. And it's not likely to work well unless it was developed and tested by people who had a pretty good idea of how to do the job right the first time. Unfortunately, instructional developers of such caliber are very few in number. Most CAI courses have been developed as if they were to be given as class lectures, and as a result they haven't turned out to be much of an improvement over the class lectures that they were designed to replace. Until we have justifiable confidence in our instructional development procedures, we would do well to leave videodisc programming in the hands of the entertainment industry.

Summary

Videodiscs will set new standards for inexpensive large-scale media distribution. They can do a lot more than provide home re-runs of TV re-runs. Educational use of videodiscs for the presentation of conventional linear motion pictures will probably catch on like "wildfire." Non-linear, interactive applications will make a real contribution to the quality of education, but *not* until instructional development becomes a matter of production, instead of experimentation.

Suggested Readings

Anonymous. Inexpensive TV Cartridges May Come from Digital Recordings. *Product Engineering*, September 1974, 13.
Anonymous. *MCA Disco-Vision.* Informational Booklet. MCA Disco-Vision, Inc., Universal City, California.
Bennion, J.L. Possible Applications of Optical Videodiscs to Individualized

Instruction. *Technical Report No. 10*. Institute for Computer Uses in Education, Brigham Young University, February 1974.

Bennion, J.L. and E.W. Schneider. Interactive Video-Disc Systems for Education. *Journal of the SMPTE, 84*(12), December 1975, 949-953.

Bounhuis, G. and P. Burgstede. The Optical Scanning System of the Philips "VLP" Record Player. *Philips Technical Review, 33*(7), 1973, 186-189.

Broadbent, K.D. A Review of the MCA Disco-Vision System. *Journal of the SMPTE, 83*, July 1974, 554-559.

Compaan, K. and P. Kramer. The Philips "VLP" System. *Philips Technical Review, 33*(7), 1973, 178-180.

Hrbek, G.W. An Experimental Optical Videodisc Playback System. *Journal of the SMPTE, 83*, July 1974, 580-582.

Janssen, P.J.M. and P.E. Day. Control Mechanisms in the Philips "VLP" Record Player. *Philips Technical Review, 33*(7), 1973, 190-193.

Jerome, J.A. and E.M. Kaczorowshi. Film-Based Videodisc System. *Journal of the SMPTE, 83*, July 1974, 560-563.

Pfannkuch, R. Characteristics of the Videodisc Systems. *Journal of the SMPTE, 83*, July 1974, 580-586.

Van der Bussche, W. *et al*. Signal Processing in the Philips "VLP" System. *Philips Technical Review, 33*(7), 1973, 181-185.

Winslow, K. A Videodisc in Your Future. *Educational and Industrial TV*, May 1975, 21-22.

Zwaneveld, E.H.A.E. An Audiovisual Producer/User's View of Videodisc Technology. *Journal of the SMPTE, 83*, July 1974, 593-584.

13.

Instructional Television: Yesterday's Magic

George N. Gordon

The co-editor of this book, Larry Lipsitz, has kindly asked me whether, as an "elder statesman" of Instructional Television, I might like to write a brief chapter on one or another aspect of this subject—and the theme of this book. He also made clear that it did not matter much whether I did or not, because he was ready to go to press with a dozen or so chapters that would be superior to anything I might have to say. As an ex-student of mine (a fact!), he probably felt an obligation at least to ask in the hope, probably, that I would refuse.

True enough, I suppose somebody should present me with a gold watch or key chain for my sheer survival. It was indeed sixteen years ago that the late Lawrence Costello and I finished the manuscript of the first "how to" book on what was then called "Educational Television." The volume was *Teach With Television*, and, as I look at the first edition of it, I notice that we suggested the substitution of the word "Instructional" for "Educational," among other things. This, I suppose, was a contribution not only to English but to the various languages into which the book was subsequently, legally and illegally, translated.

Teach With Television sold well in all editions. I lost my royalties in the stock market, and poor Costello did not live long

George N. Gordon is Professor and Chairman, Communication Arts Department, Hofstra University, Hempstead, New York.

enough to spend his. He died suddenly of a heart attack in his middle thirties after having thought up the notion—later taken by others—that people might like to watch moving pictures while sitting chairbound in an airplane on a long flight.

When the book came out, it was called "gloomy" and "pessimistic," because neither Costello nor I could generate much excitement about the Ford Foundation's early experiments with Instructional TV. We also refused to join faddists who were then touting this new technology as the solution to every problem in schooling from teacher shortages to Johnny's reading problems.

Nine years later, when I set my hand to my second book on the subject, *Classroom Television*, I was censured even more harshly for my negativism. In both instances, you see, I had had the temerity to suggest that ITV might travel in one of two possible directions: up or down. In a nation of boosters and among an educational establishment of positive thinkers, such an observation was and remains heretical. I had even, by 1969, thought up some sharp things to say about Uncle Sam and Uncle Ford and the directions they seemed to be leading all of educational technology. As a result, the U.S. Office of Education, the Ford Foundation and I all went our separate ways, which, it turned out, was fortunate.

Although none of us has yet arrived in St. Peter's domain, I think I have done much better than the USOE and Ford in the long run. At least, cold print indicates that I was a better prophet, and none of us anticipated the direction from which the body blow to our mutually idealistic aspirations for education by television eventually would come. I was afraid that ITV would fall victim both to the mediocrity that attends nearly every governmental foray into educational innovation and to the Ford Foundation's think-tank mentality that had produced, in the late fifties, schemes as cockeyed, and economically devious, as the so-called "Stoddard Plan." (Remember *that*?)

I subsequently refused a couple of well-meant invitations to join the establishment of educational Future Shock-ists and went quietly on my way in other directions. Looking backwards, it was a wise decision, made out of perversity rather than wisdom, simply because my gloom and pessimism happened to be right. Believe me, nobody in this nation—or in the world—is sadder than I am that our old ideals now lie like old bones in Death Valley, along with yellowing copies of books by Alvin Toffler and assorted cute quotations from the works of Marshall McLuhan. Like memories of Lyndon Johnson's "Great Society," they belong to a different age—separated from the present moment by a distance much greater than time alone.

Nor do I think that lost youth alone accounts for the sadness I feel as I write this. I was nearly as sad in 1960, because I was unable in good conscience to put on a funny hat and join the boosters. At the moment, I think, quite frankly, that American education on *all* levels is receiving the blow to the jugular for which it has been unwittingly asking since the end of World War II. By and large, I believe this is also a good thing, a dose of realism that is forcing us to, in the trite phrase of yesterday, "reorder our priorities." What is happening, however, is that we are reordering them sensibly by putting schooling where it belongs: somewhere beneath eating, police protection, public sanitation, transportation, energy generation and living in a relatively unpolluted environment.

And what about ITV, did someone ask? History usually tells simple stories in the long run. It died—or, at least, it went into a catatonic trance—mostly because of its successes rather than its failures. This was the eventuality that I did *not* predict, but luckily, by the time the score was in, I could not have cared less. So keep your gold watch or key chain!

I should have figured it out years ago, I see now. Ever since Comenius, and probably before, there has been no shortage of clowns, mountebanks, jugglers and recreation directors who have thoroughly convinced themselves that, given the opportunity, they would turn out to be entirely competent to teach *anything* to *anybody* better than professional teachers. After all, they know how to sell snake oil on the midway, don't they? Well, kid, why not *sell* education in the same way—not only good for man and beast but accompanied by a peek at Jo-Joe, half-man half-woman, Little Egypt and Fink's Mules.

Sad to say, these twerps are, and were, in some measure right, *half* right at any rate, except for the sly fact that they define teaching in both superficial and totally non-professional ways. They quantify what is qualitative by nature, and, like good pitchmen, they are interested in profits (or objectives) without noticing that means (or processes) is what the big game is all about. One look at the notion of ITV (and other attractive technologies whizzing about in the mid-'sixties), and how their showmen's glands salivated! Teach reading the way you sell cooking oil! Let Weber and Fields squawk morality to ghetto kids. Disnify the universe with puppets, styrofoam props and kookie costumes. Then test your audience for quantified learning. With *TV Guide* as a text book and millions in puff money for public relations, here was a "can't loose" proposition. And it cost Ford, the USOE and various passers-by only a few million bucks to get started.

I am glad that Educational Technology Publications is giving ITV a second chance. But I am not sure that it deserves one. It was inevitable that instructional video could not survive the success of *Sesame Street.* For far more complex reasons, into which I cannot go here, neither could it survive the media hype that attended Sir Kenneth Clark's "Civilisation" and Jacob Bronowski's "The Ascent of Man."

I regret this latter state of affairs more than I do the former, because Clark and Bronowski were responsible for two series of really fine television programs. But they were—and are—in the end, television programs, *not* ITV. I know a clutch of cultural illiterates who enjoyed them both, but I doubt that any fundamental educational change resulted in them from the experiences. Why should it?

Ill-conceived as educational communications (but superbly

conceived as serious, inspirational home entertainments), they seem to have left our educational landscape pretty much the same as it was before they came. Ditto *Sesame Street*. All have probably given dreary lives a bit more color than they had. But, asks the professional teacher, have they dispelled the educational miasma that foredooms formal basic education in the ghettos? Have they helped lead older minds to directed, disciplined inquiry into the past, present or future? Have they even exerted cultural forces comparable to yesterday's Chattaqua lecturers or Sunday sermons? Once the testimonials quieted down, what have they, what *could* they accomplish?

Answer the question yourself, and then decide whether or not ITV deserves a second chance. Of course, it could not survive success, American style: fallout from the Children's Television Workshop, Time-Life Films and coffee-table books for Christmas presents. Might it have survived failure? Did the answer to this question gurgle down the drain years ago, after the first semester of *Sunrise Semester* ended, the first term at Hagerstown, the first year at Anaheim or the Midwest Airborne Project? Please do not ask *me*. I am an "elder statesman."

The closest I get to ITV these days is *Mary Hartman, Mary Hartman*. Maybe this is as close as I have ever been. And maybe it is as close as I ever shall be.

14.

Improving ITV's Instructional Image

Jerrold Ackerman

Twenty years ago it was anticipated that every new school would contain a video studio and that instructional television would become an integral component of every student's learning environment. Instructional television was expected to deliver tantalizing aural and visual displays which would transform the process of education. ITV programs were to embody such visions as might be conceived by some contemporary William Shakespeare, or Leonardo da Vinci. The highest qualities of creative human expression were to merge in a constructive concert of facilitated learning.

It never happened. The image of television as a viable medium of instruction has become tarnished by a history of disappointing performances. As is typical of encounters with novel phenomena, the initial awe and enchantment with TV as an instructional medium was replaced by an "Alice-in-Wonderland" effect of frustration, disillusionment and disorientation when established logical principles failed to apply.

Violations of Expectancy:
The NSD Syndrome

Perhaps this disenchantment and disorientation were most dramatically manifested by the result of early media research efforts. For example, the anticipated instructional effectiveness of

Jerrold Ackerman holds a multidisciplinary doctorate in communications and education from the University of Texas at Austin and is currently affiliated with Mediated Instructional Systems, Orange, California.

media attributes failed to materialize. The use of color, degree of realistic detail, motion and even the visuals themselves (Baker and Popham, 1965) most often made no significant differences (NSD) in learning.

Another type of early study compared "traditional classroom instruction" to "televised instruction." In this genre of investigation, neither of the items being compared was operationalized in a manner which would permit results to be generalized. Yet, under sheer weight of numbers (Chu and Schramm, 1967, counted over four hundred separate comparisons), the usual conclusion of NSD seemed quite convincing. In such research, the content of the televised program was often the identical lecture with which the program was being compared.

According to Marshall McLuhan (1964) we ride into the future guided by images in the rear-view mirror of memory which reflects past experience. We impose old structures on new technologies: the old environment becomes the content of the new medium. As McLuhan's philosophy would predict, "traditional classroom instruction" became the content of ITV. Instead of anticipated mind-expanding images, televised instruction has all too often featured the speaker's instructionally irrelevant face. Small wonder, then, that the early history of ITV was afflicted by an NSD syndrome and the frustrations of Alice.

Those early studies did prove that televised instruction, even at its most unimaginative level, was at least as good as classroom instruction. This was scant consolation, because the cup which is half full is also seen as half empty. Why expend the time, money, effort and hassle to adopt ITV when it performs only as well as traditional classroom instruction. Clearly, "as good as" is not nearly good enough.

Thus, inability to manifest instructional effectiveness lost for ITV whatever chance there might have been to become an integral instructional component. Most often relegated to an auxiliary role, television has seldom been allowed to trespass upon the straight-and-narrow critical path of formal education.

Although television in the classroom has been no more effective than traditional instruction, John R. Silber, president of Boston University, in a recent address before the International Association of University Presidents, pictured commercial television programs as effective proselytizers of hedonism and violence. (Such a position is supported in part by the report to the Surgeon General, *Television and Growing Up: The Impact of Televised Violence*.) In other words, television is seen as transforming our entire value system. What could be more effective than that!

There are many more specific illustrations of the dramatic ability of moving-image media (i.e., film and television) to influence behavior. The dynamic mental images stirred by Orson Welles' *War of the Worlds* radiocast offered a preview of what to expect from visual media. About that time, *It Happened One Night* revealed a Clark Gable without an undershirt—which almost caused the undergarment industry to lose theirs. Shower-bathing habits in the 1950's were profoundly cut down by the film *Psycho*. In the 1970's, surfers temper their ocean-bathing behaviors with fresh images of *Jaws*.

Viewed in such contexts, the behavior-changing (i.e., learning) influences of television and film act more like fugitives from Pandora's Box than like servants of enlightenment. The problem, then, is not that TV's potentials for facilitating learning haven't been used, but that those potentials haven't been systematically channeled to constructive ends.

The following have been cited as some of the factors which underlie our failure to harness TV's instructional effectiveness:

1. We have not as yet established theoretical underpinnings for instructional media (Allen, 1973) in general or for ITV in particular. Such theoretical structures are essential to stimulate and focus productive research and to guide product development.

2. There have been few working ITV models worthy of emulation. This pertains to both educational systems with integrated TV components and to ITV programs.

3. Financial resources necessary to sustain systematic re-

search and to produce effective programs have been unreliable and frequently meager when available. Too often, the sole monetary support comes from "soft" money sources (e.g., nonrenewable funds such as government grants), since instructional television markets have been generally unattractive to investors from the private sector.

4. The disparate interests of the instructional designer and the media producer often inhibit their close cooperation and interfere with the development of mutual priorities and objectives. ITV embodies the fusion of two critical standards, those of instruction and those of television. Learner attention must be sustained but not at the expense of instructional efficiency.

Alternative Systems of Education

The systems of education which determine priorities and allocate resources control the destiny of the instructional use of television. The lack of ITV acceptance by public school systems has been described elsewhere in this volume and will not be discussed here. Much as a result of change-resisting mechanisms with the schools, *alternatives* to traditional school based educational systems have been proliferating during the past several years. The State University of Nebraska (SUN) and University of Mid-America (UMA) projects, described by Jack McBride in his current chapter on open learning delivery systems, are submitted as working models of one kind of alternative learning system (ALS).

An analysis of SUN and UMA may reveal some of the critical features of a well-planned ALS. Both SUN and UMA incorporate (1) a plan for renewable funding; (2) a total systems concept of program development (i.e., coordinated product planning, production, evaluation and implementation); (3) television (media) as a major instructional component; (4) student learning needs which are not adequately served by traditional classroom education; and (5) multiple delivery channels, many offering individualized access.

ALS have already or are about to become established in the following markets:

- Learning how to learn and printed language skills to preschool children. (Recent research indicates that moving image media would be particularly suited to these tasks.)
- Saleable vocational skills to secondary school-aged children. (This market offers a strong opportunity for a totally integrated curriculum. Mathematics and communication skills, for instance, might be learned within the context of the skill being acquired.)
- Updating professional competencies (a necessity in our technological environment and usually drudgery within traditional school systems).

Because of the interdependence of educational technology and ALS, their destinies seem to be operating in tandem.

ITV Design Concepts

What has happened in the software (or "courseware") area to warrant instructional programmers of television a second chance? The following items identify some of the concepts which have helped to reorient current approaches to ITV:

1. A medium, such as television, should be regarded more as a confluence of attributes rather than as a nondivisive entity per se (Mielke, 1968).

2. Instruction consists of critical interactions between learner, task variable, media attributes and instructional strategies (Allen, 1971).

3. Investigations have suggested that the instructional efficiency of various TV attributes (e.g., color, motion, degree of realistic detail) might be determined by relevance—that is, a given element, to be instructionally effective, must be utilized in a manner which facilitates the attainment of specific criterion objectives.

4. Theoretical and practical tenets of learning and instruction (such as programmed instruction) can be adapted and incorporated into ITV design principles and techniques.

5. Formative and summative evaluation should serve three functions in developing ITV effectiveness: (a) quality control, (b) product improvement and (c) basic research.

6. Until now, the major theoretical influence on instructional media has come from the behaviorist tradition. Many current studies indicate that even if Skinnerian principles are necessary conditions for learning, they do not constitute a sufficiency (McKeachie, 1974).

7. Sergei Eisenstein (1947) predicted that the nature of audio-visual phenomena could only be determined by studying the processes through which Man perceives and forms images of reality. Cognitive studies of perception, attention, memory, concept formation, problem-solving and imagery promise powerful implications for the instructional design of television.

8. A popular topic continues to be, "Given the instructional objectives, which medium (or media mix) is appropriate to the task and the resources available?" This approach may be practical for solving traditional schoolroom tasks but it severely limits the instructional potentials of ITV. Every medium has unique abilities to influence message content (Carpenter, 1960). Restricting objectives to those of traditional classrooms clips the wings of ITV's instructional possibilities. One might as well restrict the movement of airplanes to highway surfaces. Under such circumstances airplane performance would exhibit the no-significant-difference syndrome relative to the automobile. In terms of improving television's instructional functions, perhaps we should show more concern with the selection of objectives than of media. Rather than "Given the objectives, which medium?" a more productive approach might be, "Given television's attributes, which objectives are possible?" (Mielke, 1970).

9. Recent work suggests that educational technologists should begin to study the instructional potentials of the attribute

of *motion*. If cognitive theorists are correct (and research suggests they are), human thought processes almost surely involve dynamic transformations of information. How can the attribute of motion (which represents dynamic transformations of visual stimuli) be used to influence the dynamic transformations of thought?

Instructional Media and Imagery Theory

The literature of mental imagery offers productive insights to guide instructional media in its task of facilitating learning, and in its search for theoretical structures. Neisser (1972) identified visual mnemonic imagery as one of the most effective mental processes in learning performance.

For almost 50 years, however, the study of imagery and even discussions of mental imagery were considered taboo by most psychologists. The story of the exile and the reemergence of imagery as a respectable subject for investigation (Holt, 1964) parallels the recent rise of cognitive psychology to which imagery belongs. Allan Paivio, through his empirical yet theoretically oriented investigations, was one of the first to confer scientific legitimacy upon the study of imagery.

Starting out in the verbal learning traditions of paired-associate learning (PAL), Paivio (1963) found that noun-pairs (i.e., paired associates in which both the stimulus and response items are nouns) which had concrete nouns in the stimulus position were easier to learn than noun-pairs which had abstract stimulus nouns*. In a sustained series of investigations, Paivio and his colleagues systematically ruled out all available explanations for this facilitation except imagery** (Paivio, 1969). Thus, the image-evoking capacity of a stimulus item is said to provide an enabling context within which a response item may be assimilated, and that

---

*A noun is determined to be abstract or concrete based on the degree to which it represents objective reality. Thus, nouns such as *dog, house* and *ink* are concrete; and *justice, freedom* and *wish* are abstract.
**Imagery refers to mentally constructed representations of objective reality as perceived by any of the sensory modalities.

the mental process of imagery is the source of such facilitation. (These findings parallel the concepts of Bruner and Piaget, in which schema derived from perceptual-motor experiences underlie all human comprehension.) In a test of this "image-evoking capacity" explanation, pictures were pitted against words in paired-associate learning (PAL) tasks. Pictures were superior, especially in the stimulus position (Paivio and Yarmey, 1966; Rohwer, 1968; and Dilley and Paivio, 1968).

As is characteristic of much of the work in imagery, the above theoretical investigations studied the learning effect of pictures. For this reason, many of the experimental paradigms and theoretical constructs of mental imagery are submitted as being central to the study of instructional media. If this suggestion is cogent, educational technology may once again become a serendipitous beneficiary, this time of rigorously derived and comprehensive theoretical underpinnings which have solid foundations in human learning. In imagery studies, pictures are often used as if they supplant mental images, an approach which, as Salomon currently postulates, may also be of critical importance to learning from media, especially television.

Pictures have been extensively used as referent items (items to be learned) and as mediators (items which facilitate learning). The parameters which have been manipulated are rich and varied. For example, imagery studies (Paivio, 1971), have distinguished mediators by modality (e.g., aural, visual), by type of mnemonic strategy or organizing scheme (e.g., meaning, identification and organization of parts, analogy to familiar shapes, sound similarity such as alliteration or rhyme), by dynamic image qualities (e.g., S-R interaction, vividness, spatial organization) or by origination (e.g., self-generated by the learner or provided by the experimenter). Yet, so recently and rapidly has the rise of imagery occurred that the Levie and Dickie (1973) account of *The Analysis and Application of Media* and Levie's (1973) special issue of *Viewpoints* on the role of pictures in learning were among the first to introduce imagery as a viable construct in the research of instructional media. However, for those desiring a working knowledge, Allan Paivio's (1971) *Imagery and Verbal Processes* provides an in-depth account of the history; experimental analyses; and of theory making in progress. Although a vast amount of imagery research has been conducted since 1971, Paivio's book is so encyclopedic and well-organized that virtually all of the major issues have been delineated. Although well written, the jargon of verbal learning may make reading difficult. In this event, the reader may wish to acquire enabling context from Bugelski's (1970) *Words and Things and Images* and Bower's (1970) *Analysis of a Mnemonic Device* before attempting Paivio.

Imagery Theory Applied:
Two Media Studies

The aforementioned works are concerned with mental imagery as a construct in facilitating human learning. Most are not interested in instructional media per se, and none relate in detail to the structures of mental imagery as prospective theoretical constructs of central importance to an emerging science of instructional media design. Two studies which were conducted by the present author will be described briefly. Hopefully, some of the ways in which the mechanisms and concepts of mental imagery may be used as underpinnings for the instructional media studies may be better understood after these concrete exemplars.

The first study involved sound film as the medium to promote the learning of letter-sound associations. Although still pictures (on cards) were used in the second, its experimental results were later replicated using 35mm slides (Jordan, Ackerman, and Wicker, in press). These investigations were based upon the findings of visual imagery experiments in which item concreteness, high-stimulus imagery, interactive images,* and action pictures were all found to facilitate learning (Paivio, 1971).

*An interactive image is a mnemonic image in which two items are depicted in some kind of spatial interaction.

Study 1. The first study investigated the role of visual imagery in the learnings of 32 letter-sound associations (LSAs) by kindergarten children by varying the strength and number of visual mediators (Ackerman, 1975). Five specific questions were investigated: (1) Does mediating imagery affect learning? (2) Does mediator strength affect learning? (3) Does the number of mediating images affect learning? (4) Is there an interaction between mediator strength and number? and (5) Is there an interaction between specific letter-sound associations and mediator strength and number?

Associations to letter shapes (graphemes) and to letter sounds (phonemes) were collected from a random sample of kindergarten children. Four visual mediators for each LSA were suggested by juxtaposing the graphemic and phonemic associations (see Figure 1).

The visual mediators depicted familiar objects or concepts which resembled the letter shape and also provided a context which implied the letter sounds. For example, twin scoops of ice cream mediated the *m* - /m/ letter sound association (see Figure 2).

Under the influence of the mediator, the grapheme, *m*, acquired a concrete context (two scoops of ice cream) and the phonemic response, /m/, assumed a familiar meaning ("good" or "tastes good"). Learning was facilitated because the presentation of the letter shape *m* suggested the image of the mediator (two scoops of ice cream), which in turn implied the phoneme /m/. Theoretically, then, it may be seen that the visual mediators facilitated all three component phases (stimulus discrimination, response discrimination, associating the stimulus with the response) of paired-associate learning (PAL) as identified by Underwood and Schulz (1960).

Mediator strength was operationalized in terms of a rank-ordering test of each picture's ability to represent a particular grapheme and to infer the phoneme. For each LSA, the mediators with the best, "middlemost" and lowest scores were desig-

Figure 1

The Four Pictorial Mediators Produced
for the z-/z/ Letter-Sound Association

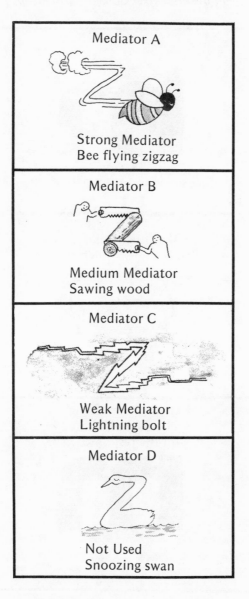

Figure 2

*Ice Cream Cone Mediator Proposed
to Facilitate the Learning of
the m-/m/ Letter-Sound Association*

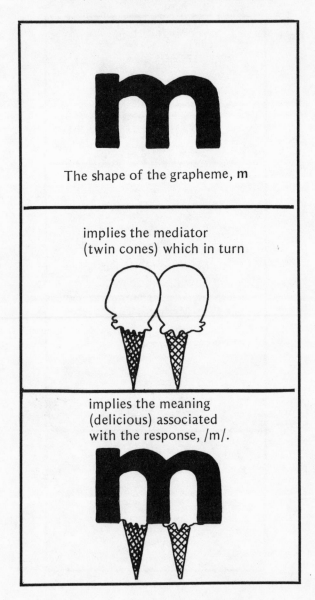

The shape of the grapheme, m

implies the mediator
(twin cones) which in turn

implies the meaning
(delicious) associated
with the response, /m/.

nated as high, medium and low strength, respectively. These were used to generate eight treatment conditions for each LSA: (1) no mediator used, (2) low, (3) medium and (4) high-strength mediators used; combinations of (5) medium and low, (6) high and low, (7) high and medium and (8) high, medium and low-strength mediators used.

The learning materials were 256 (8 treatment conditions X 32 LSAs), 37-second, 8mm sound films, identical in format.

Results. The three-mediator treatment condition performed significantly better (p < .05) than all others in the immediate, the 24-hour delayed recall and the two-week delayed recall posttests. Two mediators performed no better than one when mediator strength was controlled, and only the the strongest one- and two-mediator conditions (the high mediator and the high-medium combination) manifested statistical superiority over the no-mediator condition.

⌈It seems that mediators facilitate learning, but only if suffi- ←
ciently strong.⌉ Facilitation is almost certainly a function of mediator strength, and the number of mediators is probably a significant factor—provided that there is a sufficient number to manifest differences. Weak mediators which were slightly facilitating in themselves tended to dilute the potency of the strong mediator with which they were paired. The evidence indicated an interaction between mediator strength and number. However, the method of operationalizing mediator strength needs to be refined, and mediator number shall probably have to be varied more extensively before this relationship can be clearly seen.

Study 2. The second investigation was a pilot study which compared the effectiveness of provided pictorial (PP)* and self-generated (SG)** visual mediation across various degrees of refer-

*Pictorially provided mediation: pictorial representation of the referent items in dynamic interaction as provided by the experimenter to facilitate the learning of the S-R pairs.

**Self-generated mediation: mediation created by the experimental subject himself; in the present study, as a result of instructions to create interactive mental images.

ent item concreteness-abstractness in a PAL task.

Gordon Bower (1972) concluded that SG was more facilitative than provided mediation. However, his determination was based upon the results of several studies which used both visual and verbal SG mediation but only verbal mediation (e.g., mediating sentences) in the provided mediation treatments. No direct comparison of PP versus SG was found in the imagery literature.

In a comprehensive review of attributes which contribute to PAL tasks, Allan Paivio (1971) concluded that imagery/concreteness was the best facilitator of learning. Factor-analytic studies consistently revealed a .92 correlation between imagery and concreteness values (Paivio, 1971). Furthermore, concreteness was more facilitative on the stimulus than on the response side (Paivio, 1969). In this regard, Paivio and Yuille (1969) in a much replicated experiment found that learning, with or without mediators, was facilitated as a function of both imagery/concreteness and stimulus concreteness. Thus, learning was facilitated according to the concrete (c) or abstract (a) value of the items of S-R pairs: c-c $>$ c-a $>$ a-c $>$ a-a.

In other imagery studies, Bower (1972) and Paivio (1971) both offered extensive and convincing evidence in support of the superiority of interactive over noninteractive imagery in the visual as well as the verbal modality. Rohwer (1970) found that referent S-R nouns connected by action verbs were learned better by young children than pairs connected by prepositions and by conjunctions (e.g., The boy climbs the tree. $>$ The boy in the tree. $>$ The boy and the tree.) Epstein, Rock and Zuckerman (1960) showed that associated pictures of objects were learned better when presented in interactive conditions (e.g., pictures of a hand in a bowl, a chair under a tree) than when the items were pictorially presented as separated units. The facilitation of interaction was extended to the use of pictures as mediators by Wollen (as reported in Paivio, 1971). Thus, the learning of paired nouns (e.g., cigar-piano) was facilitated by a picture of the objects in interaction (e.g., a pictures of a cigar on a piano) more than by a picture of the objects as separate units (e.g., a picture of a cigar and a piano). Moreover, Paivio (1972) concluded that imagery-concreteness facilitation holds in the interactive condition (i.e., motion pictures > still pictures > concrete nouns > abstract nouns). Note that the dynamic interaction of motion pictures is superior to still pictures.

Extensive work has also been carried out with self-generated mediation. Bower (1972) demonstrated the superiority of self-generated over provided mediation. Subjects who were instructed to construct sentences to mediate referent items learned significantly more than subjects provided such sentences (Bobrow and Bower, 1969).

In a follow-up series of SG mediation experiments, Bower (1972) found that SG visual imagery was more facilitative than SG verbal mediation (mediating sentences). A study by Bower and Winzenz (1970) showed that a generated image of a provided sentence was more facilitative than a provided sentence alone. However, within the self-generated condition itself, the learning of concrete items was superior to the learning of abstract items.

Paivio and Foth (1970) demonstrated that mediating imagery is difficult to generate when items are abstract (low in imagery value). Not only did subjects require much more time to generate mediating visual imagery for abstract nouns, but also the visual was less effective than the verbal mediation condition and only equal to the verbal condition considering just those subjects who did manage to generate images. That concreteness can be imparted to abstract nouns through association was demonstrated by Marshal (as reported in Paivio, 1971). For example, Marshal used a picture of a baby to mediate "formula-innocence."

The present study used pictorial mediation similar to Marshal's in a test of the following hypotheses:

(1) Learning will be facilitated under PP mediation according to the concreteness-abstractness value of items of S-R pairs: c-c > c-a > a-c > a-a.

(2) Learning will be facilitated by SG visual mediation according to the concreteness-abstractness value of items of S-R pairs: c-c > c-a > a-c > a-a.

(3) PP mediation will equal SG mediation in learning facilitation with c-c pairs.

(4) PP mediation will surpass SG visual mediation in learning facilitation involving c-a, a-c and a-a S-R pairs.

(5) The superiority of PP mediation over SG visual mediation will increase from c-a to a-c pairs with the greatest superiority being recorded in the a-a pairs.

In this present PP versus SG pilot study, 64 nouns were randomly selected from the Paivio, Yuille and Madigan (1968) list (generally accepted as standard in imagery studies) of 925 nouns which had been rated for their imagery and concreteness values, such that 32 were concrete (c) and 32 were abstract (a). These nouns were randomly paired to form 32 S-R pairs such that there were eight each of c-c, c-a, a-c and a-a pairs.

Twenty-two adult subjects were randomly assigned to treatments such that there were 11 in each experimental treatment. Learning materials were thirty-two 4 X 6-inch study trial cards for each treatment condition. The SG subjects received only cards containing the items to be learned. Those subjects who were assigned to the provided pictorial condition received cards each of which contained an S-R pair of nouns to be learned and a relevant, interactive, pictorial mediator (see Figure 3).

Each card was presented for 15 seconds during the study trial. During the posttest both groups were presented the 32 stimulus words, each on a 4 X 6 card, for a period of 10 seconds per card.

Results. The results are most simply reported in terms of Figure 4, which contains the number of correct answers (the dependent measure being used in this study) obtained from each of the treatments.

Even though statistical significance was not manifested in every case, the direction of the superiority is consistent with the

Figure 3

Examples of Provided Pictorial Mediators

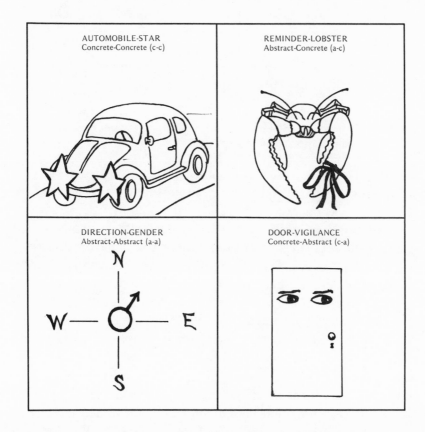

predictions in every instance. More importantly, the superiority of the provided pictorial mediation becomes increasingly stronger as the items to be learned become increasingly abstract.

A notion prevalent from the time of Sir Francis Galton holds that pictorial information may only facilitate the learning of concrete, but not abstract, concepts. This notion has persisted even though Piaget (among others) has advised that all human understanding (including abstract concepts) is rooted in representations

Figure 4

	c-c		c-a		a-c		a-a
PP	71	>	66	>	60	*>	42
			V		* V		* V
SG	72	>	61	*>	45	*>	21

*p <.01.

Comparison of the number of correct responses between provided pictorial (PP) and self-generated (SG) mediation for different levels of concrete (c) and abstract (a) paired-associate nouns.

of objective reality (such as are available through the dynamic pictorial medium of television). Even though the concept of "abstract" was operationally defined at a simplistic level, perhaps the potentials of pictorial media to facilitate abstract-concept learning and problem-solving skills may be somewhat appreciated.

Undoubtedly, many regard S-R learning with a scorn reserved for tasks which have been traditionally placed near the bottom of learning hierarchies. However, as has been repeatedly demonstrated in imagery investigations, the "S-R" in S-R learning does not stand for "simple-*rote*." The mental processes used in PAL are rich and varied, and even require strategies which parallel those used in the learning of abstract concepts. Among the advantages of initiating theoretical investigations in the locus of S-R imagery studies are experimental design simplicity, facilitated control of extraneous parameters, and the involvement of a learning skill which is recognized to be among the least complex.

In summary, there was a threefold purpose in presenting these brief examples of imagery-oriented instructional media studies:

(1) To introduce imagery concepts, literature and experimental paradigms.

(2) To describe research results of relevance to ITV presentation design.

(3) To demonstrate that imagery theory and its experimental paradigms may provide viable foundations for
investigations of instructional media.

Conclusion

This chapter has suggested approaches for upgrading television's instructional image through creative and instructionally
effective presentation design. It has also shown that the image of
ITV has several faces to improve; among the most urgent is the
talking face of instructional television, by now as much celebrated
(and ludicrous) as that jumping frog of Mark Twain.

In closing, it is suggested that optimism concerning ITV's
future be restrained. With the aid of an audiotape recording, a
certain afternoon in 1967 in Jim Finn's Instructional Technology
seminar at the University of Southern California is very clearly
recalled. The late Dr. Finn had just returned from a meeting with
representatives of various industrial complexes (e.g., RCA, IBM,
Litton, Kodak) at Los Angeles' Ambassador Hotel. The late
General David Sarnoff of RCA had just pledged his commitment
to apply the full leverage of modern systems technology to the
imperative problems confronting modern society (e.g., pollution,
energy, transporation) and to education in particular. Dr. Finn
allowed as how he had seen Industry blow hot and cold before,
but that interest and commitment had at last seemed to be gen-
uine. Thus, Dr. Finn predicted that with such high priority, the
job would be accomplished "within the decade." That was in
1967.

The decade is gone and with it went the leadership of Dr.
Finn and General Sarnoff. With them went whatever hopes there
might have been for full-scale Industrial participation in developing the instructional power of television within the past ten years.

With self-sustaining systems of educational technology just
aborning, with the commercial introduction of the videodisc still
months away, and with theoretical structures of instructional
media not much more than a twinkle in our conceptual eye,

another ten years may be required to establish only a *beginning* toward a long anticipated Golden Age of Instructional Television.

References

Ackerman, J. The Strength and Number of Visual Mediators in Learning Letter-Sound Associations in Reading: A Film Study. Unpublished doctoral dissertation, University of Texas at Austin, 1975.

Allen, W. H. Instructional Media Research: Past, Present and Future. *AV Communication Review*, 1971, *19*, 5-18.

Allen, W. H. What Do 50 Years of Media Research Tell Us? *Audiovisual Instruction*, 1973, *18*, 48-49.

Baker, E. L. and W. J. Popham. Value of Pictorial Embellishments in a Tape-Slide Instructional Program. *AV Communication Review*, 1965, *13*, 397-404.

Bobrow, S. A. and G. H. Bower. Comprehension and Recall of Sentences. *Journal of Experimental Psychology*, 1969, *80*, 455-461.

Bower, G. H. Analysis of a Mnemonic Device. *American Scientist*, 1970, *58*, 496-510.

Bower, G. H. Mental Imagery and Associative Learning. In L. Gregg (Ed.) *Cognition in Learning and Memory*. New York: John Wiley, 1972.

Bower, G. H. and D. Winzenz. Comparison of Associative Learning Strategies. *Psychonomic Science*, 1970, *20*, 119-120.

Bugelski, B. R. Words and Things and Images. *American Psychologist*, 1970, *25*, 1002-1012.

Carpenter, E. The New Languages. In E. Carpenter and M. McLuhan (Eds.) *Explorations in Communication*. Boston: Beacon Press, 1960.

Chu, G. C. and W. Schramm. *Learning from Television: What the Research Says*. Washington: National Association of Educational Broadcasters, 1967.

Dilley, M. G. and A. Paivio. Pictures and Words as Stimuli and Response Items in Paired-Associate Learning in Young Children. *Journal of Experimental Child Psychology*, 1968, *6*, 231-240.

Eisenstein, S. *The Film Sense*. New York: Harcourt, Brace and World, Inc., 1947.

Epstein, W., I. Rock and C. B. Zuckerman. Meaning and Familiarity in Associative Learning. *Psychological Monographs*, 1960, *74* (Whole No. 491).

Holt, R. R. Imagery: The Return of the Ostracized. *American Psychologist*, 1964, *19*, 254-264.

Jordan, E., J. Ackerman and F. Wicker. Comparison of Provided Pictures and Self-Generated Visual Imagery. In press.

Levie, W. H. (Ed.). Research on Learning from Pictures: A Review and Bibliography. *Viewpoints: Bulletin of the School of Education, Indiana University*, 1973, *49* (2).

Levie, W. H. and K. E. Dickie. The Analysis and Application of Media. In R. M. Travers (Ed.) *Second Handbook of Research on Teaching*. Chicago: Rand McNally, 1973, 858-882.

McKeachie, W. J. The Decline and Fall of the Laws of Learning. *Educational Researcher*, March 1974, 7-11.

McLuhan, M. *Understanding Media: The Extensions of Man*. New York: Signet Books, 1964.

Mielke, K. W. Questioning the ETV Question. *Educational Broadcasting Review*, 1968, *2*, 6.

Mielke, K. W. Media-Message Interactions in TV. In G. Salomon and R. E. Snow (Eds.) Commentaries on Research in Instructional Media: An Examination of Conceptual Schemes. *Viewpoints: Bulletin of the School of Education, Indiana University*, 1970, *46* (5), 15-31.

Neisser, U. Changing Conceptions of Imagery. In Sheehan, P. W. (Ed.) *The Function and Nature of Imagery*. New York: Academic Press, 1972.

Paivio, A. Learning of Adjective-Noun Paired Associates as a Function of Adjective-Noun Word Order and Noun Abstractness. *Canadian Journal of Psychology*, 1963, *17*, 370-379.

Paivio, A. Mental Imagery in Associative Learning and Memory. *Psychological Review*, 1969, *76*, 241-263.

Paivio, A. *Imagery and Verbal Processes*. New York: Holt, 1971.

Paivio, A. The Role of Imagery in Learning and Memory. In Sheehan, P. W. (Ed.) *The Function and Nature of Imagery*. New York: Academic Press, 1972.

Paivio, A. and D. Foth. Imaginal and Verbal Mediators and Noun Concreteness in Paired-Associate Learning: The Elusive Interaction. *Journal of Verbal Learning and Verbal Behavior*, 1970, *9*, 384-390.

Paivio, A. and A. D. Yarmey. Pictures Versus Words as Stimuli and Responses in Paired-Associate Learning. *Psychonomic Science*, 1966, *5*, 235-236.

Paivio, A. and J. C. Yuille. Changes in Associative Strategies and Paired-Associate Learning Over Trials as a Function of Word Imagery and Type of Learning Set. *Journal of Experimental Psychology*, 1969, *79*, 458-463.

Paivio, A., J C. Yuille and S. Madigan. Concreteness, Imagery and Meaningfulness Values for 925 Nouns. *Journal of Experimental Psychology*, 1968, *76* (1 Pt. 2).

Rohwer, W. D., Jr. Socioeconomic Status, Intelligence and Learning Proficiency in Children. Paper presented at the meeting of the American Psychological Association, San Francisco, Sept., 1968.

Rohwer, W. D., Jr. Images and Pictures in Children's Learning: Research Results and Instructional Implications. In H. W. Reese (Chm.) Imagery in Children's Learning: A Symposium. *Psychological Bulletin*, 1970, *73*, 393-403.

Underwood, B. J. and R. W. Schulz. *Meaningfulness and Verbal Learning*. Chicago: Lippincott, 1960.

Appendix
Instructional Television:
Recent Research

Warren F. Seibert

The instructional uses of television—and it is troublesome but true that in some sense all uses thus qualify—have developed impressively since a quarter century ago, when educators first took note of television and began to experiment and seek roles for it. No one then foresaw television's rapid spread, a spread that involves not only geography but forms or styles and influence as well. Thus, television today is not just everywhere. It is also doing, attempting to do or perceived as doing all manner of things. And in the process it is using a wide array of methods, strategies and technical arrangements, with still others certain to come.

Seen through the eyes of an optimist these developments can appear a success story with few parallels in history. Imagine, within a quarter century a global television society has been created and, by individual choices, includes a population which now numbers in the hundreds of millions, if not billions. Moreover, some within this society can hardly distinguish between their television and their lives. They use the medium gullibly and to excess. Television has reached the point where it affects people's lives in ways that were once reserved for long established,

This Appendix is reprinted—with the permission of the ERIC Clearinghouse on Information Resources, Stanford Center for Research and Development in Teaching, School of Education, Stanford University—from *Instructional Television: The Best of ERIC,* published in July, 1976. **Warren F. Seibert** is with the Measurement and Research Center, Purdue University.

major social institutions. And television's particular far-reaching effects upon the young, whose personalities are the most quickly and profoundly affected, remain largely a mystery.

Thus, not all of television's developments fit a pattern of success and clear promise. Instead, the medium has failed to live up to certain hopes and expectations. It has become a source of unwanted main and side effects. And, possibly the most serious of all, it has pointed up our own failures to gauge well and to anticipate such effects. We still understand the medium only superficially.

It might therefore be said that the development of television and its roles provides a story with important parallels to that other prominent technology which originated during the same earlier era, atomic energy. Both have proliferated quickly, both are unquestionably potent, and as a result, both require the most thoughtful policies and stewardship. Both are attractive for their many potential benefits and alarming for their dangers, and we are destined to spend our lives with both whether or not we learn to use them wisely.

The foregoing provides a perspective for considering television research generally and instructional television research in particular. Such research is clearly essential, and a great deal of it, too, if we are to learn enough to guide the wise use of this revolutionary medium. Some progress is being made, as we think the contents of the following pages will confirm. But the remaining tasks and responsibilities belong among the most difficult ones.

About This Paper's Structure

The abstracts were sorted into nine categories (plus *Other*) on the basis of two principal considerations. First, I have some feeling for the several communities of interest that our colleagues represent and I tried to arrange annotations so that each of these communities could find information it might want. Secondly, I performed what is sometimes called an "eyeball cluster analysis," i.e., a purely subjective set of judgments for the purpose of maximizing both the homogeneity within clusters and the "distance" between clusters.

Probably the best justification can be given for the first cluster, *Children and Television*, since so many people express a primary interest in this topic. These abstracts seem generally to reflect interests that encompass the full breadth of childhood, of TV uses, and of its effects; and furthermore, much good work is done in this field. The second topic, *Influencing Skills and Attitudes*, comes close to being a "school television" category, but that label could not accommodate the main thrust of certain publications which otherwise belonged. *Policy and Funding* would seem to speak for itself.

The *Programming Research and Evaluation* category has much formative and summative work within it, but I broadened it to accommodate other studies, such as Danowski's, Krull's and Mielke's. *Satellite and Cable Systems* is included primarily because there appears to be a fair-sized community of individuals with major interest in these systems and their development. *Television Effects, General* was needed to catch those publications which were left over from *Influencing Skills and Attitudes* and *Programming Research and Evaluation*. *Television for Adult Audiences* has a justification like that of *Satellite and Cable Systems*—a distinct audience exists for reports on the topic.

The *Bilingual Education* category reflects much interest in this area, but has only two unique entries. Finally, the *Television in a Foreign Setting* category is one that has seemed especially interesting to me for some years now, and also to others in the field. I believe it is justified by what it can uniquely provide by way of natural experiments and schemes which from our rather parochial view can be too easily overlooked.

Children and Television

Ball, Laurie A. *Study of the Effects of "Sesame Street" and "Polka Dot Door" on Preschool Children*. April 1974. 83pp. ED 105 970.

A study was designed to determine whether children's intelligence scores and their parents' attitudes toward preschool television programs affected the children's reactions to "Sesame Street" and "Polka Dot Door." Results of parental response to a questionnaire and observation of the children's behavior before, during and after viewing the two programs indicated that: (1) the effect of television was significant and created a more parallel pattern across behaviors in the case of "Sesame Street"; (2) parents' positive attitudes toward television did not correlate significantly with children's overt reactions; and (3) the theory that the more intelligent the child, the more quantitatively he or she will react to the television was accepted for "Sesame Street" but rejected for "Polka Dot Door." The report includes a review of the literature.

Ball, Samuel, and others. *Reading with Television: An Evaluation of The Electric Company. A Report to the Children's Television Workshop. Volumes 1 and 2*. New York: Children's Television Workshop; Princeton, New Jersey: Educational Testing Service, February 1973. 200pp. ED 073 178.

These two volumes provide an evaluation of "The Electric Company's" first year of broadcasting. Included in Volume 1 are sections on the evaluation method, results, and a summary of project activities and future research. Sample questionnaires are included in the appendix. Volume 2 gives the supporting data for the study.

Berkman, Dave. *Descriptions of Children's Television Series Produced Under the Emergency School Aid Act (P.L. 92-318)*.

Washington, D.C.: Bureau of School Systems, Division of Equal Educational Opportunity Program Operations, 1974. 9pp. ED 108 667.

This paper lists and describes twelve separate educational television program series of varying lengths. A fact sheet explains the production and evaluation of the public service spot announcements which inform young viewers that these shows can be seen on the Public Broadcasting Service network.

Cagno, Dick, and Joe E. Shively. *Children's Reactions to Segments of a Children's Television Series. Technical Report Number 34.* Charleston, West Virginia: Appalachia Educational Laboratory, June 1973. 30pp. ED 093 357.

An observational evaluation study coded 3-, 4- and 5-year-old children's responses to and behavior during daily TV lessons. The program, "Around the Bend," had a format paced to permit children to respond to instructions. A number of different programming techniques were used. The study found that providing interesting and appealing programming seems to be based upon variety and short segments.

Children's Television Workshop Annual Report 1973. New York: Children's Television Workshop, September 1973. 40pp. ED 088 428.

An open letter from the president of the Children's Television Workshop (CTW) summarizes the Workshop's previous successes, its goals and its financial situation and difficulties. The major elements of CTW's research and development laboratory and the successes of "Sesame Street," both in the United States and abroad, are reviewed. Details documenting the classroom impact of "The Electric Company," the ultimate impact of the community education services offered by CTW, and the extension of the curriculum through other non-broadcast media also are discussed.

The Children's Television Workshop; How and Why It Works. Final Report. Jericho, New York: Nassau County Board of Cooperative Educational Services, 1973. 219pp. ED 086 203.

> The organizational principles which CTW used to provide leadership, to develop functional relationships among the segments of a large-scale enterprise and to harness research to creative ends are illustrated.

Cooney, Joan Ganz. *Children's Television Workshop. Progress Report.* New York: Children's Television Workshop, August 1974. 13pp. ED 095 892.

> During July through September of 1973 the Children's Television Workshop (CTW) evaluated old material and planned new programming. A nationwide research study indicated that "The Electric Company" was watched by 3.5 million students. The series meets its reading instruction objective. No general changes in its curriculum were planned, but there were to be some changes in emphasis. "Sesame Street's" new programming was to give fuller treatment to the bilingual/bicultural area, as well as to emotions and feelings.

Cosgrove, Michael, and Curtis W. McIntyre. *The Influence of "Misterogers Neighborhood" on Nursery School Children's Pro-social Behavior.* Paper presented at the Southeastern Conference of the Society for Research in Child Development, Chapel Hill, North Carolina, March 1974. 15pp. ED 097 974.

> The impact of "Misterogers Neighborhood" on nursery school children's prosocial behavior was assessed. Two hypotheses were tested: (1) that children who viewed several "Misterogers Neighborhood" programs would evidence more prosocial behavior than would nonviewers, and (2) that young viewers would show an increase in prosocial behavior greater than that shown by older viewers. The results indicated that children viewing network programming de-

signed to teach prosocial behavior can benefit by viewing. However, no support was obtained for the second hypothesis.

Ellis, E.N., and others. *The Impact of "Sesame Street" on Primary Pupils in Vancouver*. British Columbia: Vancouver Board of School Trustees, Department of Planning and Evaluation, July 1972. 34pp. ED 077 988.

Questionnaires were directed to parents of children in eight kindergartens and to 34 elementary school principals in Vancouver to determine with what regularity the children viewed "Sesame Street" and "The Electric Company," and the impact of these programs on learning. A comparison of test scores revealed that regular viewers of "Sesame Street" had superior knowledge and understanding of letters, words, numerals, quantities and shapes. Their teachers claimed that the regular viewers had derived other important benefits, such as observational skills, more awareness of their surroundings, broader interest, greater sensitivity and consideration for others.

Felsenthal, Norman A. *Sesame Street: Socialization by Surrogate*. Paper presented at the Speech Communication Association Meeting, Chicago, Illinois, December 30, 1974. 11pp. ED 105 987.

Portions of "Sesame Street" programs which contribute to children's learning of socially acceptable attitudes and behaviors were examined in detail. Comparisons were made between "Sesame Street" programs aired during the initial 1969-70 season and a sampling of more recent program segments.

Liebert, Roland J. *"The Electric Company" In-School Utilization Study. Volume 2: The 1972-73 School and Teacher Surveys and Trends Since Fall 1971*. Tallahassee: Florida State University, Institute for Social Research; Durham, North Carolina: Research Triangle Institute, Statistics Research Division, October 1973. 238pp. ED 094 775.

This second-year study of in-school use of "The Electric Company" television series provides information on the technical capabilities of schools to use television, on applications of educational television, and on the attitudes of students, teachers, school administrators and the educationally-involved public toward television as an instructional medium. The results of three mailed surveys of elementary school principals and teachers showed that in-school utilization expanded considerably in most areas of the nation, with the series being used by an increasingly diversified range of schools.

MacDonald, Margery A. *Evaluation of ITV: Electric Company Pilot. Research Report Number 7210.* Syracuse, New York: Syracuse City School District, May 1972. 17pp. ED 090 955.

Specific objectives were to find ways to measure: (1) the degree to which the media presentation's objectives were being met, and (2) the appeal of the show, as judged by viewers' attention. The study involved five intermediate grade level educable mentally retarded (EMR) students who viewed three segments of "The Electric Company." The results were inconclusive, due to small sample size and the sophistication of the viewers vis-a-vis the show.

Palmer, Edward L. *The Deer and the Duck.* New York: Children's Television Workshop, 1973. 6pp. ED 078 938.

This response to the criticism of "Sesame Street" by Herbert A. Sprigle in the December 1972 issue of *Childhood Education* maintains that Sprigle misconstrued and misrepresented the program's mandate and objectives, and that the design and reporting of his study are so flawed that his conclusions are virtually meaningless.

Searcy, Ellen, and Judith E. Chapman. *The Status of Research in Children's Television.* Washington, D.C.: Interagency Panel on

Early Childhood Research and Development, January 1972. 142pp. ED 086 355.

> To provide a synthesis of the status of research on children's television that could be used as an information base for planning purposes, an outline of critical television research topics which need further investigation was compiled from an analysis of major reference documents and personal interviews. Selected state-of-the-art documents also were reviewed. A comparison is made between research needs and research activity.

Singer, Dorothy G., and Jerome L. Singer. *Family Television Viewing Habits and the Spontaneous Play of Pre-School Children.* Paper presented at the American Psychological Association Meeting, New Orleans, Louisiana, August 30-September 3, 1974. 21pp. ED 101 855.

> This research study examined ways in which exposure to a children's television show, "Misterogers Neighborhood," would enhance the spontaneous imaginative play of children after several weeks. The first phase of the project involved a comparison of three groups of preschool children in a day care center and regular meetings with parents to obtain data on television viewing habits and on parents' attitudes toward sex role in child rearing and toward personal and social self-worth. The second phase of the investigation involved observing the children during the "Misterogers" programs to see what kinds of materials held their attention. Intervention procedures included the establishment of parent groups that met through the following year to provide help in learning to use the television medium more effectively. Findings for each phase of the project and its implications are presented.

Singer, Jerome L., and Dorothy G. Singer. *Enhancing Imaginative Play in Preschoolers: Television and Live Adult Effects.* 1974. 38pp. ED 100 509.

A study explored the possibility that exposure to the "Misterogers Neighborhood" program might increase the likelihood of spontaneous imaginative play in preschool children who watched the program over a period of two weeks. The investigation was to determine whether a well-produced professional program would be more effective in enhancing imaginative play than instruction from a live adult. Results suggest that children in the 3- to 4-year-old age group remain most susceptible to influence by a concerned adult in their presence. It is likely that television's prosocial or optimal cognitive benefits may have to depend on some mediation by an adult.

Starkey, John D., and Helen Lee Swinford. *Reading? Does Television Viewing Time Affect It?* DeKalb: Northern Illinois University, 1974. 12pp. ED 090 966.

Some 226 fifth and sixth graders were the subjects of this study to correlate amount of television viewing and reading scores. Researchers found that (1) the average viewing time per week for girls was 28 hours and for boys 30 hours; (2) better readers watched less television than poor readers; and (3) no relationship was shown between a child's access to a private television and his or her viewing time or reading ability. The report discusses other studies of the influence of television on children and concludes that a child should be taught to be a discriminating television viewer.

A Study of the Messages Received by Children Who Viewed an Episode of "The Harlem Globetrotters Popcorn Machine." New York: Child Research Service, Inc., Columbia Broadcasting System, Inc., Office of Social Research, April 1975. 75pp. ED 108 697.

Some 687 children, aged 7 through 11, were interviewed to determine the extent to which "The Harlem Globetrotters Popcorn Machine" television programs communicated prosocial messages. Among the findings were: (1) overall, 87 percent of the children received one or more specific pro-social messages; (2) older children (10-11) were more likely to play back at least one pro-social message than were younger children (7-8), and middle class children were more likely to do so than lower class children; (3) reception of pro-social messages was not related to frequency of viewing the "Globetrotters"; and (4) "slippage" was indicated by the fact that 35 percent of the children inaccurately stated that the "Globetrotters" taught them to play basketball or to spell.

Thomas, Sally A. *Violent Content in Television: Effect of Cognitive Style and Age in Mediating Children's Aggressive Responses*. Paper presented at the American Psychological Association Convention, Honolulu, Hawaii, September 2-3, 1972. 2pp. Available from American Psychological Association, 1200 17th Street, Washington, D.C. 20036. ED 072 845 (microfiche only).

Results of this study investigating the impact certain cognitive styles have in mediating the influence of aggressive television on young boys supported the premise that the effect of TV exposure depends not only on the content but also on the child's cognitive style and way of responding to the environment in general. Younger children were found to be significantly more aggressive than older children, and the level of cognitive functioning was more differentiated, organized, elaborated and articulated as a function of maturity.

Influencing Skills and Attitudes

Chu, Godwin C., and Wilbur Schramm. *Learning from Television: What the Research Says. Revised Edition*. Washington, D.C.: National Association of Educational Broadcasters; Stanford,

California: Stanford University, Institute for Communication
Research, 1975. 135pp. Available from National Association of
Educational Broadcasters, 1346 Connecticut Avenue, N.W., Washington, D.C. 20036 ($4.00 members, $6.00 non-members). ED
109 985.

This broad survey examines a variety of aspects relating to
television's effectiveness in the classroom. An introductory
essay identifies significant trends that have emerged since the
original publication of this report in 1967. Sections cover (1)
the generalized effects of TV on pupil learning; (2) what has
been learned about the efficient use of TV in a school
system; (3) analysis of 30 variables important to the
effectiveness of televised teaching; (4) staff and student
attitudes toward television use; and (5) educational television
in developing nations. The effectiveness of instructional radio
and other media in the learning process is also briefly
considered.

Cosgrove, Michael. See **Children and Television.**

Ellis, E.N. See **Children and Television.**

Hornik, Robert C. *Television, Background Characteristics and
Learning in El Salvador's Educational Reform.* Stanford, California: Stanford University, Institute for Communication Research, April 1974. Paper presented at the American Educational
Research Association Meeting, Chicago, Illinois, April 15-19,
1974. 19pp. ED 089 678.

The use of instructional television (ITV) as part of an
educational reform in grades 7, 8 and 9 in El Salvador had a
positive effect upon learning, despite inequities in cognitive
skills related to student background and inequities in
resource distribution. In addition, students in schools using
ITV showed greater achievement than their counterparts in
schools without ITV. These results ran counter to findings in

the United States, where background factors continue to dominate over innovations.

Klees, Steven J. *Television and Other Determinants of Scholastic Achievement in Mexican Secondary Education.* Stanford, California: Stanford University, Institute for Communication Research, April 1974. Paper presented at the American Educational Research Association Meeting, Chicago, Illinois, April 15-19, 1974. 64pp. ED 090 937.

Research was conducted to compare the efficacy of the Mexican Telesecundaria (TS) system, which used instructional television (ITV), with that of the Ensenanza Directa (ED), which employed traditional instructional techniques. Results indicated that ITV had a significant positive effect on achievement; this effect was sufficiently strong to overcome other disadvantages associated with the TS system, such as larger class size and adverse student background factors. In addition, the costs of the TS system were 25 percent lower than those of the ED. It was concluded that it was technically and economically feasible to implement the TS system.

Liebert, Roland J. See **Children and Television**.

Nolan, Jeanne, and John Gross. *Mulligan Stew; An Evaluation of the Television Series.* Columbia: Missouri University, Extension Education Department, February 1975. 23pp. ED 105 889.

To evaluate the effects of the public television series on nutrition, "Mulligan Stew," a survey was conducted of 4332 fourth, fifth and sixth grade students in four areas of Missouri. Comparisons were made between teacher-reinforced lessons and no reinforcement, and children were questioned whether they believed additional programs would be helpful. Children who watched the program at school scored higher in posttest nutrition knowledge; girls scored higher than boys, and fourth and sixth graders higher than fifth. Teacher reinforcement significantly increased nutrition knowledge. Both teachers and students evaluated the series positively.

Reich, Carol, and Alan Meisner. *A Comparison of Colour and Black and White TV*. Ontario: Toronto Board of Education, Research Department, October 1972. 33pp. ED 072 655.

While previous studies on the relative effectiveness of color vs. black-and-white television concentrated on the factual retention of subject matter, this study was designed to thoroughly analyze subjective attitudes as well. Researchers tested 12 seventh grade classes at experimental Toronto schools. The study found that there was little evidence that color was a different instructional medium than black-and-white. The data suggested that color may reduce the value of the spoken word, making color a valuable medium when the material to be taught involves visual experience or a dramatic event.

Report of Television Multi-Channel System in Lincoln Heights Elementary School. Progress Report. Cincinnati, Ohio: WCET-TV, September 1973. 27pp. ED 084 844.

A comprehensive television and videotape system was installed in the elementary school in Lincoln Heights, Ohio to improve the academic performance of the school's students, who previously had been underachieving. The program was flexible, teacher controlled and attracted staff commitment. Existing shows and teacher-designed programs were used as integral parts of the instructional effort. Preliminary test results indicated significant improvement in student achievement, particularly in language arts.

Salomon, Gavriel. *Annual Report of the First Year of Research on Cognitive Effects of Media*. Israel: Hebrew University of Jerusalem, September 1974. 13pp. ED 105 969.

This paper discusses the rationale for a cross-cultural (Israeli-American) study to examine: (1) the extent to which exposure to television has an effect on children's mastery of cognitive skills; and (2) the extent to which activities of "encoding" (activities through which children communicate their ideas via television or film) have instructionally desirable effects on the mastery of cognitive skills. Two versions of an experimental film and a battery of measures were developed as part of the study.

Singer, Dorothy G., and Jerome L. Singer. See **Children and Television**.

Singer, Jerome L., and Dorothy G. Singer. See **Children and Television**.

Stein, Aletha Huston, and Lynette Kohn Friedrich. *Prosocial Television and Young Children's Behavior: Learning from Prosocial Television; Effects of Rehearsal on Performance Measures*. Paper presented at the American Psychological Association Convention, New Orleans, Louisiana, August 30-September 3, 1974. 16pp. ED 103 113.

Two studies investigated the impact of prosocial TV programs and rehearsal techniques on children's learning or acquisition of program content and on performance of behavioral adoption. Subjects were 73 kindergarten boys and girls who saw four "Misterogers" programs or four neutral programs on consecutive school days, followed by 15-20 minute training sessions. Two types of rehearsal were explored for children who saw the prosocial programs: verbal labeling and role playing. In the second study, a measure was taken of the children's inclination to engage in helping behavior in an experimentally controlled classroom situation. Findings indicated: (1) both types of training (verbal labeling and role playing) following prosocial television enhanced learning and performance of prosocial content; (2) verbal labeling had the greatest impact on verbal measures, particularly learning for girls; (3) role playing was more effective, particularly for boys, in facilitating the performance of nonverbal helping behavior; and (4) the combined training condition often led to elevated scores for both sexes.

A Study of Messages Received by Children Who Viewed an Episode of "The Harlem Globetrotters Popcorn Machine." See **Children and Television**.

Tate, Eugene D., and Stuart H. Surlin. *A Cross-Cultural Comparison of Viewer Agreement with Opinionated Television Characters.* Paper presented at the International Communications Association Meeting, Chicago, Illinois, April 1975. 12pp. ED 106 884.

> To test the relationship between dogmatism and agreement with the television character Archie Bunker among adult Canadians, researchers hypothesized that highly dogmatic Canadians would demonstrate the same identification with Archie Bunker that highly dogmatic viewers from the U.S. demonstrate, and that Canadians would not view "All in the Family" as being true to life. Two random samples were drawn from adults in two university communities— Saskatoon, Saskatchewan and Athens, Georgia. Both hypotheses were confirmed.

Thomas, Sally A. See **Children and Television**.

Policy and Funding

Compensation for TV College Studio Teaching and Supporting TV Instruction, Appendix B.3. Chicago, Illinois: Chicago City Colleges, Learning Resources Laboratory, 1974. 5pp. ED 091 028.

This excerpt from "Agreement" 1973-1975 outlines the two-year contract between the Board of Trustees of Community College District No. 508, County of Cook and State of Illinois, and the Cook County Teachers Union.

Evaluation of the Market for Instructional Television and the Effects of Changes in the Communications Industry. Current and Potential Use of ITV. Final Report. Volume 1. Princeton, New Jersey: Mathematica, December 1973. 152pp. ED 100 300.

This study to develop information for the Department of Health, Education and Welfare concluded that the role of ITV in secondary schools is expected to remain limited in the near future. However, it has an important role to play in the home where real incentives exist for purchase of video-delivered education, especially in continuing and adult education. Success in attempts at implementation will depend upon the extent of coordination achieved among educators in a research, advisory and evaluative role; producers in a creative and distributive role; and institutions in an accrediting and certification role. The report makes a number of recommendations for implementation.

Evaluation of the Market for Instructional Television and the Effects of Changes in the Communications Industry. Delivery Systems. Final Report. Volume 2. Princeton, New Jersey: Mathematica, December 1973. 246pp. ED 100 301.

This volume of a study for the Department of Health, Education and Welfare provides a detailed description of alternative delivery systems. It analyzes the different technical capabilities and component costs of a variety of distribution system configurations, including cable television, pay television, closed-circuit television, video disc, video tape, UHF broadcasts, microwave systems, satellite systems and computer-assisted instruction systems. A basis for cost comparison is described. The report notes that although the technology described exists, much of it has not gone beyond the demonstration stage.

Morris, Charles R., and others. *Public Access Channels: The New York Experience*. New York: Center for Analysis of Public Issues, CATV Project, March 1972. 64pp. ED 089 706.

A New York City cable television (CATV) project carried out by the Center for Analysis of Public Issues for the Fund for the City of New York attempted to analyze and determine what might be done to encourage the development of public access television, i.e., CATV channels allocated for use by the public. The report concludes that broadly-based usage will occur only if (1) greater audience penetration is achieved; (2) viewers adopt interactive rather than passive attitudes toward CATV; and (3) better technical equipment and financing are obtained.

Tressel, George W., and others. *The Future of Educational Telecommunication; A Planning Study*. Columbus, Ohio: Battelle Memorial Institute, Columbus Laboratories, 1975. 130pp. Available from Lexington Books, D.C. Heath and Company, 125 Spring Street, Lexington, Massachusetts 02173 ($11.00). ED 105 876.

The status and goals of educational broadcasting were examined by surveying the literature and broadcast facilities in order to help plan for the future of ETV. A summary predicts less formal education support for public broadcasting and suggests ways this might be affected. Appendixes list stations and groups contacted.

Programming Research and Evaluation

Barrington, Harold. *The Instructional Effectiveness of Television Presentation Techniques*. Ormskirk, England: Edge Hill College, Centre for Instructional Communications, January 1972. 19pp. ED 097 916.

Closed circuit television equipment was used to produce two versions of a program on the psychology of learning for use with student teachers. Program A was designed in accordance with the suggestion that the more a presentation approximates reality, the more effective it will be. The theory behind Program B was that a presentation will be more effective if the information is "precompressed" before transmission. The findings indicated that the "precompressed" procedure was more effective than the "realism" procedure.

Brooke, Martha L., and others. *A Team Approach to Developing an Audiovisual Single-Concept Instructional Unit*. Bethesda, Maryland: American Physiological Society, July 1974. 8pp. ED 102 967.

In 1973 the National Medical Audiovisual Center undertook the production of several audiovisual single-concept teaching units. This paper describes the procedure used in producing one of these units, "Left Ventricle Catheterization." The systematic team approach to instructional media development was judged an effective strategy for media production, since it required a pooling of the varied talents of team members.

Cagno, Dick. See **Children and Television**.

Danowski, James A. *Alternative Information Theoretic Measures of Television Messages: An Empirical Test*. Paper presented at the Association for Education in Journalism Meeting, San Diego, California, August 18-21, 1974. 30pp. ED 096 686.

This research examines two information theoretic measures of media exposure within the same sample of respondents and examines their relative strengths in predicting self-reported aggression. The first measure is the form entropy (DYNUFAM) index of Watt and Krull, which assesses the structural and organizational properties of specific television messages, and the second is a content entropy measure developed by the author, which indexes the entropy of respondents' exposure to categories of television programs. The results of the analyses, compared by using linear analysis models, indicate that the form entropy measure has higher predictive power than the content entropy measure in relationships with agression.

Flaugher, Ronald L., and Joan Knapp. *Report on Evaluation Activities of the Bread and Butterflies Project*. Princeton, New Jersey: Educational Testing Service, October 1974. 103pp. ED 097 921.

An evaluation of the "Bread and Butterflies" series of 15 television programs on career development for 9- to 12-year-olds sought to answer these questions: Was the program appealing to the students? Did the students comprehend the program? Were the educational objectives met by the television program alone? Were the educational objectives met by the television program plus the classroom activities? The series was proclaimed successful only if the goal was to provide an affective stimulus. No effect was observed on the achievement of specific and particular behaviorally-defined educational objectives.

Friedlander, Bernard Z. *The Communicative Effectiveness of Television as a Teaching Medium in the Elementary School Classroom: A Program of Investigation*. West Hartford, Connecticut: Hartford University, Infant/Child Language Research Laboratory, March 1974. 10pp. ED 105 853.

A proposed research program would establish a standard method of evaluating the effectiveness of educational television programs for elementary school students. Because research shows that children's comprehension and cognitive assimilation of skills, facts and ideas is a far more intricate and problematical process than has previously been supposed, and because of the extremely high costs of quality television production, it is important to have a standard method of evaluating the television curriculum.

Friedlander, Bernard Z., and Harriet S. Wetstone. *New England Instructional Television Research Center (NETREC)*. West Hartford, Connecticut: Hartford University, July 1975. 36pp. ED 109 981.

The objectives, rationale and program of NETREC are defined, along with methods of formative evaluation during production. Seven videotest research projects cover methods of evaluating communicative effectiveness of primary-grade educational television (ETV); methods for determining pre-school children's comprehension of ETV programs; effects of format, soundtrack and children's age on comprehension; appropriateness of age/grade designation; and evaluation of a bilingual program, "Mundo Real."

Katzman, Natan. *One Week of Public Television, April 1972. Number Seven*. Washington, D.C.: Corporation for Public Broadcasting, May 1973. 96pp. Available from Corporation for Public Broadcasting, Information Systems Office, 1111 Sixteenth Street, N.W., Washington, D.C. 20036. ED 078 691.

This report analyzes four types of programming: instructional programming, Children's Television Workshop productions, news and public affairs programming, and general audience programming. Data are presented concerning various characteristics of the broadcasters such as amount of time broadcasting, type of program presented, source of distribution of programming, budget size of broadcaster, region of the country, type of license and size of population served. A summary shows that the Public Broadcasting Service's programs and locally produced programs increased in usage, that there was an increase in instructional programming, and that the quality of programming appeared to improve.

Krull, Robert, and others. *Program Entropy and Structure: Two Factors in Television Viewership*. Paper presented at the International Communication Association Meeting, New Orleans, Louisiana, April 17-20, 1974. 41pp. ED 097 741.

This study compared an information processing-based measure of television program form to a measure of form based on the perception of the organization of program production elements. Three hypotheses were set up to test the presumption that the two program measures are related to the same underlying dimension: show scores for entropy and structure were expected to be correlated, viewing and liking of both measures of program form was expected to be non-random in the same way, and differences in viewing and liking patterns were expected to be similar. The DYNUFAM scores for program form entropy and the structure measures of program organization were found to be correlated at a statistically significant level, and it appears that two measures of program form are tapping the same underlying dimensions. One hypothesis failed to receive support: although liking of both measures of program form was expected to be non-random so that programs were tightly clustered, the data indicated that the opposite is true.

Laosa, Luis M. *Carrascolendas: A Formative Evaluation*. Los Angeles: University of California, March 1974. 203pp. ED 090 968.

A formative research project sought to test viewer reactions to two pilot programs of the "Carrascolendas" series. A total of 360 Puerto Rican-American, Cuban-American, Mexican-American and Anglo-American children in grades 1, 2 and 3 were observed as they watched the programs. Results indicated that there was high eye contact during the presentation and that viewers frequently smiled and laughed. Posttests showed that, on the average, students comprehended and recalled two-thirds of the material.

MacDonald, Margery A. See **Children and Television**.

Mielke, Keith W. *Decision-Oriented Research in School Television*. Bloomington, Indiana: Agency for Instructional Television, September 1973. 23pp. ED 082 536.

A review of the contributions of evaluation to school television and policy suggestions for evaluation programs are offered to help the Agency for Instructional Television (AIT) use evaluative research. Four categories of decision-oriented research are identified—background, formative, summative and policy. Major recommendations include: (1) each AIT activity should have a research and evaluation component; (2) AIT should focus upon decision-oriented and product-specific research and evaluation; and (3) summative research, while necessary, is less important than formative research.

O'Bryan, K.G. *Monkey Bars Research Report. Report No. 46*. Toronto: Ontario Educational Communications Authority, Research and Planning Branch, 1974. 84pp. Available from Ontario Educational Communications Authority Publications, P.O. Box 19, Station R., Toronto, Ontario M46 323, Canada ($1.50). ED 098 974 (microfiche only).

A study of 64 Canadian 7- to 12-year-olds and of adults who might influence their television viewing habits measured the receptivity and acceptability of "Monkey Bars," a children's television program created as an alternative for Saturday morning viewing. Results showed that younger children overall enjoyed the program, but were not able to grasp all its humor as older children could. Appendixes include the original observation sheets, questionnaires and interview schedules.

Searcy, Ellen, and Judith E. Chapman. See **Children and Television**.

Singer, Jerome L., and Dorothy G. Singer. See **Children and Television**.

A Study of Messages Received by Children Who Viewed an Episode of "The Harlem Globetrotters Popcorn Machine." See **Children and Television**.

Van Wart, Geraldine. *Evaluation of a Spanish/English Educational Television Series Within Region XIII. Final Report. Evaluation Component*. Austin, Texas: Education Service Center Region 13, June 1974. 234pp. ED 092 089.

> This fourth year evaluation reports the effects and usage of "Carrascolendas," a children's television series in Spanish and English. Research conducted in Texas schools encompassed three phases: a field experiment to measure learning effects; attitudinal surveys among teachers, parents and children; and a process evaluation of the Education Service Center Carrascolendas staff members. Viewers made a significant gain score increase in the Spanish areas of history, culture and reading, and in the English areas of history, culture and science. The content areas which had the least impact in Spanish and English were math and self-concept. Attitude items on which viewers made significant gains over non-viewers dealt with speaking Spanish and teacher approval of schoolwork.

Satellite and Cable Systems

Bramble, William J., and others. *Education on the Beam: A Progress Report on the Appalachian Education Satellite Project*. Lexington, Kentucky: Appalachian Education Satellite Project,

April 1975. Based on a paper presented at the American Educational Research Association Meeting, Washington, D.C., April 1, 1975. 23pp. ED 108 660.

> The Appalachian Regional Commission (ARC) saw the sixth Applied Technology Satellite (ATS-6) as a means of improving the quality of inservice teacher education by distributing high quality courses from a central source. Fifteen classroom sites were scattered from New York to Alabama. There were four major learning activities: (1) 30-minute, pretaped television programs which included lectures, interviews and demonstration teaching; (2) audio reviews of the pretaped television programs; (3) live seminars which allowed students to ask questions of their teachers and other experts; and (4) resource libraries at each site. This National Institute of Education-sponsored report includes one-page summaries on: evaluation strategies, how well did the equipment work, how well did the system for relaying seminar questions work, what were the participants like, how well did the participants like the different learning activities, how much did the participants learn, did the participants become convinced of the values of course concepts and procedures, are the teachers using the skills learned, and conclusions.

Carlson, Robert. *Possibilities and Limitation of Cable TV for Adult Education*. Paper presented at the Federal City College Conference on Cable TV, Washington, D.C., April 1974. 8pp. ED 096 392.

> To the extent that educators, local governments and the public can serve the interests of capitalism and the entrepreneur—and only to that extent—will educators, local governments and the public have an opportunity for access to privately controlled cable TV. The author encourages educators, minority groups, municipalities and other such public interests to struggle for control of cable systems.

Design for an Analysis and Assessment of the Education Satellite Communications Demonstration: Final Report. Washington, D.C.: Practical Concepts, Inc., May 1974. 433pp. ED 093 330.

A three-month evaluation design effort developed a strategy and implementation plan for a policy level evaluation of the Educational Satellite Communications Demonstration (ESCD). This report, sponsored by the National Institute of Education, covers: (1) development of the evaluation strategy and plan; (2) data collection and analysis; (3) measurement of the impact of satellite TV on the way educational institutions are perceived; (4) measurement of the impact of satellite TV on educational institutions and behavior toward them; and (5) calibration of use that is made of satellite TV.

Educational Uses of Cable Television. Washington, D.C.: Cable Television Information Center, 1974. 110pp. Available from Cable Television Information Center, The Urban Institute, 2100 M Street, N.W., Washington, D.C. 20037. ED 097 878 (microfiche only).

The educational uses of cable television and the methods and problems of those uses are described in a state of the art review. Federal Communications Commission regulations and related franchise activity are described, and the methods of using the educational channel as open or closed circuit TV or pay TV are indicated for different types of students, the community, the school and general information needs. The appendixes contain discussions of television markets, innovative educational uses of cable television, equipment, schools and programs.

Forsythe, Charles, and Earl Cardellino. *Cable Television and Education: A Position Paper. Based On the Proceedings of the Pennsylvania Learning Resources Association Sponsored CATV and Education Conference, Seven Springs Mountain Resort, Champion, Pa., May 11-12, 1973.* Latrobe: Pennsylvania Learning

Resources Association, January 1974. 12pp. Available from
Pennsylvania Learning Resources Association, Mr. Charles G.
Forsythe, Harvey House, 1525 Ligonier Street, Latrobe, Pennsyl-
vania 15650. ED 088 468.

> Cable television (CATV) has often been put to educational
> uses too quickly, too comprehensively, too superficially and
> for the wrong reasons. In Pennsylvania, as in other states,
> there is a need for a systematic approach to coordinating
> CATV with other educational resources. The Pennsylvania
> Department of Education can promote more effective use of
> cable by: (1) identifying the educational needs which can be
> served by CATV; (2) maintaining current information on
> available cable facilities; (3) designing a plan to provide cable
> channels to education; (4) encouraging the development of
> educational programming; (5) providing evaluation services
> for cable-related activities; and (6) fostering research on new
> uses of CATV.

*The Here, Now and Tomorrow of Cable Television in Education:
A Planning Guide.* Boston: Massachusetts Advisory Council on
Education, September 1973. 75pp. ED 086 172.

> In order for the potential of cable television to be applied for
> educational benefit, educators must effectively communicate
> their priorities and needs to both licensing authorities and
> cable companies. This guide familiarizes educators and school
> committees with their options and prepares them to take part
> in local franchise negotiations. Throughout all parts of the
> book, it is emphasized that a cable system should be designed
> and operated to fit the particular structure and needs of a
> local community.

Morris, Charles R., and others. See **Policy and Funding**.

Molenda, Michael. *Instructional Television in Higher Education.*
Bloomington: Indiana University, January 1974. Paper presented

at the Conference on Cable Television and the University, Dallas, Texas, January 29-31, 1974. 11pp. Available from Proceedings of the Conference on Cable Television, EDUCOM, P.O. Box 364, Princeton, New Jersey 08540 ($6.00). ED 093 387.

> Research evidence indicates that at-home TV students tend to perform better than their on-campus counterparts and they frequently have a more favorable attitude toward learning via the TV. Cable offers at least two unique technical capabilities: (1) multiple channels for simultaneous communications with multiple small audiences; and (2) two-way interaction between the teacher and the learner. In essence, educators must decide what they want cable to do for institutions.

Niemi, John A. *Possibilities and Limitations of Cable TV for Adult Education*. Paper presented at the Federal City College Conference on Cable TV, Washington, D.C., April 1974. 16pp. ED 096 394.

> The paper investigates various organizational models of cable TV ownership and control, legislation in Canada and the United States regarding cable systems, and the potential of cable as an information network for adult education. Cable TV is a valuable resource for the adult educator, and, in an era when people feel alienated, provides an opportunity to focus on community issues and relate more personally with the viewer. Limitations regarding the use of cable TV for adult education include: (1) the problem of control, (2) lack of trained staff, (3) unimaginative programming, (4) lack of funds, (5) limited time available for citizen programming, (6) lack of audience involvement, and (7) lack of research.

Walkmeyer, John E., Jr., and others. *Market Scenarios and Alternative Administrative Frameworks for U.S. Educational Satellite Systems. Memorandum No. CG-75/2*. St. Louis, Missouri: Washington University, Center for Development Technology, April 1975. 170pp. ED 107 268.

Intended as a framework for analysis of the costs and benefits of developing an operational educational satellite system in the United States, this memorandum presents a series of scenarios of potential applications together with alternative organizational arrangements to support them. The number of satellite channels (25) and the number of ground terminals (up to 50,000-70,000) that might be required to serve various educational sectors are estimated.

Television Effects, General

Atwood, L. Erwin, and Keith R. Sanders. *Perceived Dimensions of Political Campaign Communication*. Paper presented at the International Communication Association Meeting, New Orleans, Louisiana, April 17-20, 1974. 33pp. ED 098 643.

Advocates of the "new politics" have argued that television for political campaigning can be effectively used to encourage and enhance the probability of split ticket voting. Derivation and analysis of seven perceived dimensions of political campaign communication among registered voters finds television unrelated to voting behavior. The print media dimension and media believability discriminate among voter groups.

Cater, Douglass, and Stephen Strickland. *A First Hard Look at the Surgeon General's Report on Television and Violence*. Washington, D.C.: Academy for Educational Development, Inc.; Palo Alto, California: Aspen Institute for Humanistic Studies, Program on Communications and Society, March 1972. 12pp. ED 081 175.

In March 1972 the Aspen Program on Communications and Society convened a meeting of the Surgeon General, staff members connected with the Surgeon General's *Report on Television and Violence*, and social scientists to evaluate the *Report*, which had just been issued. This conference report summarizes the background of concern over violence on television, discusses the genesis and composition of the Advisory Committee which undertook the project, describes the research and the *Report*, treats its significance, and considers some approaches to public policy.

Danowski, James A. See **Programming Research and Evaluation.**

Kreimer, Osvaldo. *Open, Sesame: A Key to the Meaning of the Educational Broadcast Message*. Stanford, California: Stanford University, Institute for Communication Research, December 1974. 51pp. ED 102 964.

Research findings, theories and examples of the effectiveness of radio and television programs are organized to create a guide for analyzing their educational messages. It is demonstrated that radio and television programs are composed of a set of messages made up of more than one level of language, such as verbal (words), paraverbal (pitch, intonation) and analogic (sounds analogous to real ones), and that these levels interact with each other to create a multidimensionality which not only gives meaning to the message but can also jeopardize or distort the expected results.

LeRoy, David J., and others. *Mediated Violence and Victim Consequences: A Behavioral Measure of Attention and Interest*. Tallahassee: Florida State University, Communication Research Center, July 1974. 18pp. ED 101 712.

Using a modified television set that required them to depress a foot pedal in order to view the material, 77 subjects watched a nonviolent segment of the film, "The Chase," and either a violent sequence with consequences to the victim or violence without consequences. Subjects were randomly assigned to each treatment on the basis of Buss-Durkee Aggression scores. Allowed to choose to respond or not to respond to the material, 58 percent of the subjects chose not to attend at the rate necessary to continually view the program. No relationships were found between the subject's Buss-Durkee score and the subject's behavior elicited by the stimulus materials.

Starkey, John D., and Helen Lee Swinford. See **Children and Television**.

Television for Adult Audiences

Blakely, R.J. *Use of Instructional Television in Adult Education: A Review of Some Recent Developments*. Syracuse, New York: ERIC Clearinghouse on Adult Education; Syracuse University, Publications Program in Continuing Education, January 1974. 32pp. Available from Publications in Continuing Education, Syracuse University, 224 Huntington Hall, Syracuse, New York 13210 ($1.50). ED 089 076.

This paper, concerned with criteria for using instructional television, calls attention to some developments that may not be familiar to adult educators. The author describes an evolving discipline divided on the meaning of "instructional technology" (gadgetry or systems approach?), and reviews the findings of research on instructional television as they apply to adult education. Several specific situations where ITV is used effectively are used as examples. The author concludes that "there is no point in trying to do what most instructional television programming for adults has tried to do," and he offers his own guidelines for adopting televised instruction.

Carlson, Robert A. *Educational Television in Its Cultural and Public Affairs Dimension: A Selected Literature Review of Public Television as an Issue in Adult Education. Occasional Papers Number 39*. Syracuse, New York: ERIC Clearinghouse on Adult

Education; Syracuse University, Publications Program in Continuing Education, December 1973. 50pp. Available from Publications in Continuing Education, Syracuse University, 224 Huntington Hall, Syracuse, New York 13210 ($2.00). ED 086 890.

> This booklet reflects the continuing controversy in the field of adult education over the place that adult educators should accord to noncommercial cultural-informational television (Public Television or PTV). Viewing some of the notions in adult education that discourage acceptance of PTV as a unique broadcast form of education, this study analyzes the concerns arising from these notions. Based on this analysis "the review will argue that if the values of adult education were to achieve dominance in Public Television, independent-minded Americans would be much the worse off for such 'progress.' " More than half of the booklet is devoted to an annotated bibliography, which is divided into two parts: The Conflicting Hopes and The Reality.

Compensation for TV College Studio Teaching and Supporting TV Instruction, Appendix B.3. See **Policy and Funding.**

Lefranc, Robert. *The Combined Use of Radio and Television and Correspondence Courses in Higher Education. (European University and Post-University Distant Study Systems.)* Strasbourg, France: Council for Cultural Cooperation, 1973. 58pp. Available from Council for Cultural Cooperation, Council of Europe, Strasbourg, France ($6.00). ED 093 247.

> The original subject of this study was the combined use of radio/television with correspondence courses in higher education. It has been broadened to take in all multimedia distant study systems at the postsecondary level, in consequence of the general intrinsic development of these systems, in which radio/TV and correspondence courses are less and less frequently the only media used. The analyses contained in

this book concentrate on those systems already in operation or projected that have been studied by the Council of Europe.

Molenda, Michael. See **Satellite and Cable Systems**.

Perraton, Hilary, and others. *The International Extension College, 1972-1973. Second Annual Report*. Cambridge, England: International Extension College, 1973. 22pp. ED 093 302.

The purposes of the International Extension College are the facilitation of nonformal education in the Third World using three-way teaching—the integrated use of correspondence, broadcasting and face-to-face tuition. The major project implementing these goals is the Mauritius College of the Air. Other smaller or less-developed projects in Botswana, Lesotho, Nigeria, other African countries and Bangladesh are described, along with the activities of the Home Office in England to provide information, training and research.

Report on the Stanford Instructional Television Network. Academic Years, 1969-70 Through 1972-73. Stanford, California: Stanford University, Stanford Instructional Television Network, February 1974. 8pp. ED 087 382.

The Stanford Instructional Television Network has completed four years of operation, broadcasting some 160 hours of live instruction per week over four Instructional Television Fixed Service channels. The Network was designed as an interactive system with a two-way FM audio link between the student in off-campus classrooms and the instructors at Stanford. The Network has experienced an excellent growth of membership, with 34 industry and four educational organizations affiliated. Originally the ratio was 85 percent credit-seeking to 15 percent non-credit students; now 28 percent of the students are seeking credit with 72 percent participating in the non-credit categories.

Zigerell, James J., and Hymen M. Chausow. *Chicago's TV College: A Fifth Report*. Chicago, Illinois: Chicago City Colleges, Learning Resources Laboratory, January 1974. 38pp. ED 089 806.

> This is the final report to be issued with a 1956 grant to the City Colleges of Chicago for the development of instructional television. The 18 years of the TV College's operation are covered under the following topics: (1) Making the Walls Fall, (2) The Overall View, (3) Education Continuing—and Available, (4) Students and Teachers, (5) Getting Courses on Camera, (6) Extending the Classroom Even Further, and (7) A Final Word.

Television for Bilingual Education

Laosa, Luis M. See **Programming Research and Evaluation**.

Van Wart, Geraldine. See **Programming Research and Evaluation**.

Williams, Frederick, and others. *Carrascolendas: National Evaluation of a Spanish/English Educational Television Series. Final Report*. Austin: University of Texas, Center for Communication Research, June 1973. 416pp. ED 078 679.

> A field experiment, attitude surveys and a process evaluation were conducted in order to evaluate the third year of "Carrascolendas," a kindergarten-second grade bilingual series carried nationwide on the Public Broadcasting Service. Test scores showed that material presented in Spanish had a significant impact on learning in history and culture. Attitudes of teachers, parents and children toward the series were positive, and a growth of pride in Mexican culture was noted. The process evaluation found improvement in the management of the project, although insufficient dissemination of information about the series to potential viewers was regarded as a salient shortcoming.

Wolf, Judith G., and David Sylves. *Evaluation of a Bilingual Television Series, Villa Alegre: Final Report*. Buffalo: State University of New York, Buffalo College at Buffalo, Educational Research and Development Complex, 1974. 65pp. ED 103 511.

This evaluation study determined students' and classroom personnel's reactions to "Villa Alegre"—a television series produced by Bilingual Children's Television, Inc.—in order to ascertain whether this series would be a worthwhile addition to bilingual classrooms. Some 135 students and 23 adults participated in two bilingual summer school projects. Responses from three surveys were extremely positive. On this basis, it would seem that the series would be a worthwhile addition to bilingual classrooms.

Television in a Foreign Setting

Educational Broadcasts of NHK. Special Issue of NHK Today and Tomorrow. Tokyo: Japan Broadcasting Company, March 1975. 35pp. ED 107 247.

A special issue of *NHK Today and Tomorrow*, published by Japan Broadcasting Company, describes open-circuit and classroom broadcasts. Policies of NHK are explained and standards are listed for educational programs in general, school programs, children's programs and cultural programs. Programs of correspondence education for senior high school and for higher education are described. A full explanation is given of the social education programs, including foreign language lessons, vocational and technical lessons, programs related to agriculture, forestry and fisheries, programs for children, programs for women, programs for business management, science programs and cultural programs. A brief history of NHK is appended.

The First ETV Project of Turkey. Eskisehir, Turkey: Eskisehir

Academy of Economic and Commercial Sciences, 1974. 20pp. ED
090 991.

> The success of a small-scale, closed circuit educational
> television project run at the Academy of Economic and
> Commercial Sciences in Eskisehir, Turkey has led to the
> expansion of the experiment. The expanded project will offer
> services to other academies, demonstrate the effective use of
> educational television, and serve as an integral part of
> Turkey's Third Five-Year Development Plan for education.
> Lectures will be broadcast to large and scattered groups of
> students, and videotapes will be prepared and exchanged with
> other institutions both in Turkey and throughout Europe.

Hawkridge, David G. *The Open University's Role in a Democracy*.
Paper presented at the Leidse Onderwijsintellingen Jubilee
Congress, The Hague, Netherlands, October 1973. 11pp. ED 083
830.

> The steps which led to the establishment of the Open
> University in Great Britain and the intentions of its founders
> are described. Following this is an examination of the
> University's success in reaching its target student population.
> The third section of the paper provides an analysis of the
> instructional system of the University and the place of
> correspondence materials within that system.

Hornik, Robert C., and others. *Television and Educational Reform
in El Salvador. Final Report*. Stanford, California: Stanford
University, Institute for Communication Research, August 1973.
183pp. ED 084 810.

> Stanford University's Institute for Communication Research
> was asked in 1968 to conduct an evaluation of a new
> instructional television (ITV) system in El Salvador. The first
> chapter identifies the context of the evaluations. The second
> chapter presents the results of four years of research on
> learning, while the third chapter presents a picture of student

attitudes across the four years of research. Students' educational and occupational aspirations are summarized in the fourth chapter, and background information of the students, their schools and their communities is presented in the fifth chapter. The next few chapters report studies of teacher attitudes and behavior, studies of the efficiency and cost of the system, and an administrative history of ITV. A final chapter discusses alternative strategies for the use of instructional technology to expand educational opportunity.

Hornik, Robert C. See **Influencing Skills and Attitudes.**

Ingle, Henry T., and others. *Television and Educational Reform in El Salvador. Report on the Fourth Year of Research. Research Report Number Eleven*. Stanford, California: Stanford University, Institute for Communication Research, May 1973. 146pp. ED 077 219.

Studies of the instructional television (ITV) system of El Salvador and its educational reform program for 1972 are summarized. ITV moved into new facilities and the program was increasingly run by native personnel. General ability and reading scores increased, although there was little difference between television and non-television classes. Students were enthusiastic about ITV, but teacher enthusiasm waned somewhat after the initial uncritical acceptance.

Klees, Steven J. See **Influencing Skills and Attitudes.**

Mayo, Judith A. *Teacher Observation in Mexico*. Stanford, California: Stanford University, Institute for Communication Research, May 1973. 41pp. ED 077 220.

A comparative study was made of Mexican secondary teachers in the Telesecundaria (TS), which utilizes televised instructional programs, and in the Ensenanza Directa (ED), which does not. The following implications seemed warranted: (1) the educational level of the individual should be a criterion for selection as a teacher; (2) teachers should .provide students with an introduction to televised instructional programs to encourage fuller participation; (3) teachers should spend more time in planning their classes; and (4) teacher training should prepare teachers to rely less on lecturing and more on activities which stress individualized learning, student participation and group work.

Salomon, Gavriel. *Effects of Encouraging Israeli Mothers to Co-observe Sesame Street With Their Five-Year-Olds.* Jerusalem: Hebrew University of Jerusalem, September 1973. 24pp. ED 086 174.

Research examined the learning effects of encouraging Israeli mothers to co-observe "Sesame Street" with their five-year-olds. A total of 93 kindergarten children, drawn about equally from lower and middle class families, was divided between mothers' encouraged and non-encouraged conditions. Encouraging mothers had a profound effect on the amount the lower socio-economic status (SES) children watched the show. This in turn had an effect on their learning.

Schramm, Wilbur. *Instructional Television in the Educational Reform of El Salvador. Information Bulletin Number Three.* Washington, D.C.: Academy for Educational Development, Information Center on Instructional Technology; Stanford, California: Stanford University, Institute for Communication Research, March 1973. 96pp. Available from Information Center on Instructional Technology, Academy for Educational Development, 1424 Sixteenth Street, N.W., Washington, D.C. 20036. ED 074 763.

In 1967, El Salvador initiated a comprehensive educational reform centering around the use of instructional television (ITV) in grades 7, 8 and 9. Other aspects of the reform included extensive teacher retraining, curriculum revision and extensive building of new schoolrooms, among other things. Classes with all aspects of the reform (including ITV) evidenced only slightly higher learning gains than did classes with all aspects of the reform except ITV. Thus the role of ITV in improving achievement is inconclusive.

Schramm, Wilbur. *ITV in American Samoa—After Nine Years.* Stanford, California: Stanford University, Institute for Communication Research, March 1973. 63pp. ED 077 189.

This is the first report on the instructional television (ITV) project in American Samoa based on any considerable amount of hard data. Experimental evidence shows that the longer pupils in any given grade had been exposed to television, the better their English performance. Attitudes toward instruction by television decline sharply in the upper grades and high school, and between elementary and high school teachers. It is possible that after teaching standards rise (in part because of ITV itself), students and teachers become impatient with the mass and central control of the broadcasts.

Other

Basic Statistics on Instructional Television and Other Technologies; Public Schools, Spring 1970. Washington, D.C.: National Center for Educational Statistics (DHEW/OE), February 1973. 5pp. ED 084 776.

Information is presented for all public schools, by elementary and secondary levels. Statistics indicate that 75 percent of all schools have TV, 26 percent have VTRs, 22 percent have both, and 21 percent have neither VTRs or TV. Other significant findings include the facts that 82 percent of all pupils are in schools with TV, that more than 70 percent of the schools with TV use educational television, and that the median number of TV sets per school is two.

Borton, Terry, and others. *Dual Audio Television: The First Public Broadcast*. Philadelphia, Pennsylvania: Philadelphia School District, Office of Curriculum and Instruction, 1974. 19pp. ED 094 753.

  A study was conducted in conjunction with the first publicly announced broadcast of dual audio television—a new method of combining simultaneous radio instruction and commercial entertainment TV. The results indicated that dual audio could attract 24 percent of the target age range children watching the TV show, that it was practical as far as the TV station and parents were concerned, and that there was a positive correlation between number of days listened and test scores. These results, confirming data collected in a number of previous studies, indicate that dual audio is now sufficiently developed so that its effectiveness as a mass medium should be tested over a full broadcast season.

Bretz, Rudy, and others. *Models of Television-Based Educational Programs: A Draft Report. A Working Note*. Santa Monica, California: Rand Corporation, August 1971. 87pp. ED 088 488.

  The study examined the developmental steps which preceded the production of "Sesame Street" by Children's Television Workshop, of the Chicago TV College, of Telekellog of Germany and of the "Advocates." The aim was to identify developmental models to be used in connection with the creation of a new career education program aimed at women in the home and sponsored by the United States Office in Education. If a program can be based upon an existing organization, if it requires neither extensive research nor complex programming, and if objectives, target audience and methods are known in advance, then an effective television-based educational program can be developed in a short time.

Chapman, Dave, and Frank Carioti. *Design for ETV: Planning for Schools with Television. Revised*. Chicago, Illinois: Chapman

Design, Inc.; New York: Educational Facilities Laboratories, Inc., 1968. 97pp. Available from Educational Facilities Laboratoires, Inc., 477 Madison Avenue, New York, New York 10022 ($2.00). ED 072 518.

The study results reflect seven years' review by a design team experienced with educational and instructional television as developed by teachers and administrators from "scratch" and of the requirements and use of television in school situations. The report offers verbal and visual comments, recommendations and suggestions as guides for those involved in school planning and school space design. Listings of representative references and a glossary of ETV terms conclude the report.

Educational Media and Technology: Publications from ERIC at Stanford 1967-1973. An ERIC Bibliography. Stanford, California: Stanford University, ERIC Clearinghouse on Information Resources, August 1974. 17pp. ED 093 350.

All 59 documents published by the Educational Resources Information Center on Educational Media and Technology (ERIC/EM) are abstracted in this document.

Guide Book 1975; Television Instruction. Bloomington, Indiana: Agency for Instructional Television, 1975. 38pp. ED 098 997.

The videotape courses available through the Agency for Instructional Television (AIT) are listed. Courses fall into three broad categories: primary through senior high, postsecondary and teacher inservice. The policies, procedures and prices for use of videotape courses are provided. As an aid to the potential user of instructional television materials, professionally-oriented publications and films distributed by AIT are listed. The document also contains historical notes on the development of AIT and its predecessor organization, National Instructional Television, together with a list of the current AIT professional staff and board of directors.

Kreimer, Osvaldo. See **Television Effects, General**.

Low, D. Stewart. *The Instructional Development Factory*. Provo, Utah: Brigham Young University, Institute for Computer Uses in Education, February 1973. Paper presented at the American Educational Research Association Meeting, New Orleans, Louisiana, February 25-March 1, 1973. 39pp. ED 074 749.

The large-scale development of Time-Shared, Interactive, Computer-Controlled, Information Television (TICCIT) at Brigham Young University is described. The project incorporated a combination of computer terminals and television consoles that were able to provide the learner with a complete instructional system. This paper discusses the relationships between the general elements of the system: design, training, courseware and management. The system is unique because it incorporates industrial techniques into a large instructional system.

1975 Recorded Visual Instruction. Lincoln: University of Nebraska, Great Plains National Instructional Television Library, 1975. 197pp. ED 100 323.

The 1975 catalog lists recorded visual materials available through the Great Plains National (GPN) Instructional Television Library in Lincoln, Nebraska. Series and materials descriptions are provided together with the following indexes: (1) elementary, by subject matter; (2) 4-H series; (3) elementary, by grade level; (4) junior high, secondary, and adult; (5) utilization and inservice; (6) college; and (7) special products. General information on usage policies, prices, previewing, and the GPN staff is also included.

Park, Ben. *An Introduction to Telemedicine; Interactive Television for Delivery of Health Services*. New York: New York University, N.Y. Alternate Media Center, June 1974. 265pp. ED 110 028.

This paper explores the technical, psychological and cultural aspects of telemedicine—the use of two-way or interactive television to conduct transactions in the field of health care. Pioneer systems providing communication between central facilities and remote locations are described, along with 20 ongoing and proposed projects. The paper examines the method's capabilities in aiding general diagnosis, cardiology, dermatology, radiology, psychiatry, mental retardation and speech therapy.

Documents with ED numbers listed in this Appendix may be ordered from the ERIC Document Reproduction Service (EDRS), P.O. Box 190, Arlington, Virginia 22210. Documents without ED numbers may be ordered from the source given in the citation.